Making Meaning for Operations

Casebook

A collaborative project by the staff and
participants of Teaching to the Big Ideas

Principal Investigators

Deborah Schifter
Virginia Bastable
Susan Jo Russell

with
Lisa Yaffee
Jill Bodner Lester
Sophia Cohen

Dale Seymour Publications®
Parsippany, New Jersey

National Science Foundation

This work was supported by the National Science Foundation under Grant Nos. ESI-9254393 and ESI-9050210. Any opinions, findings, conclusions, or recommendations expressed here are those of the authors and do not necessarily reflect the views of the National Science Foundation.

Additional support was provided by the Massachusetts Higher Education Coordinating Council and the Dwight D. Eisenhower Mathematics and Science Education Program.

Published by Dale Seymour Publications®, 299 Jefferson Road, Parsippany, NJ 07054

Dale Seymour Publications® is an imprint of Addison Wesley Longman, Inc.

EXECUTIVE EDITOR: Catherine Anderson
PROJECT EDITOR: Beverly Cory
PRODUCTION/MANUFACTURING DIRECTOR: Janet Yearian
SENIOR PRODUCTION/MANUFACTURING COORDINATOR: Fiona Santoianni
DESIGN DIRECTOR: Phyllis Aycock
DESIGN MANAGER: Jeff Kelly
TEXT AND COVER DESIGN: Paula Shuhert
COMPOSITION: Joe Conte

Many of the designations used by manufacturers and sellers to distinguish their products are claimed as trademarks. Where those designations appear in this book, and Dale Seymour Publications was aware of a trademark claim, the designations have been printed in initial caps.

Cuisenaire® is a registered trademark of the Cuisenaire Company of America, Inc.

Multilink™ is a trademark of NES Arnold, Ltd.

Unifix® is a registered trademark of Philograph Publications, Ltd.

ISBN 0-7690-0172-6
DS21964

2 3 4 5 6 7 8 9 10 <ML> 03 02 01

This product is printed
on recycled paper

Teaching to the Big Ideas

Developing Mathematical Ideas (DMI) was developed as a collaborative project by the staff and participants of Teaching to the Big Ideas, an NSF Teacher Enhancement Project.

PROJECT DIRECTORS   Deborah Schifter (EDC), Virginia Bastable (SummerMath for Teachers), Susan Jo Russell (TERC)

STAFF   Sophia Cohen (EDC), Jill Bodner Lester (SummerMath for Teachers), Lisa Yaffee (TERC)

PARTICIPANTS   Allan Arnaboldi, Lisa Bailly, Audrey Barzey, Julie Berke, Nancy Buell, Yvonne Carpio, Rose Christiansen, Ann Connally, Nancy Dostal, Marcia Estelle, Becky Eston, Trish Farrington, Victoria Fink, Gail Gilmore, Nancy Horowitz, Debbie Jacques, Marcy Kitchener, Rick Last, Eileen Madison, Joyce McLaurin, Rena Moore, Amy Morse, Deborah O'Brien, Marti Ochs, Anne Marie O'Reilly, Hilory Paster, Jessica Redman, Priscilla Rhodes, Margie Riddle, Jan Rook, Doug Ruopp, Sherry Sajdak, Cynthia Schwartz, Karen Schweitzer, Lisa Seyferth, Susan Bush Smith, Diane Stafford, Liz Sweeney, Nora Toney, Polly Wagner, Carol Walker, and Steve Walkowicz, representing the public schools of Amherst, Belchertown, Boston, Brookline, Lincoln, Newton, Northampton, Pelham, South Hadley, Southampton, Springfield, Westfield, and Williamsburg, Massachusetts, and the Atrium School in Watertown, Massachusetts

VIDEO DEVELOPMENT   Susan Jo Russell, Judy Storeygard, David Smith, and Megan Murray (TERC)

CONSULTANTS, *MAKING MEANING FOR OPERATIONS*   Deborah Ball (University of Michigan), Jere Confery (University of Texas at Austin), Megan Franke (UCLA), Erick Smith (University of Illinois at Chicago), John P. (Jack) Smith III (Michigan State University)

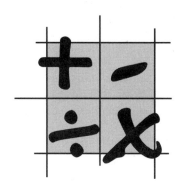

C O N T E N T S

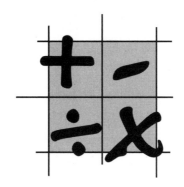

Introduction

Making *Meaning for Operations* is Part 2 of a two-part seminar exploring the teaching of number and operations to elementary and middle school students. Part 1, *Building a System of Tens,* explores the structure of the base ten number system and how children come to understand it. Among the questions considered in Part 1 are these: What is it that children must already understand when they invent their own computational methods? What is it that they come to understand as they invent such methods? In addressing these questions, the cases in *Building a System of Tens* look most closely at issues related to place value. However, those cases also provide glimpses into children's thinking about the meaning of the operations.

Thus, in case 17 in *Building a System of Tens,* second grader Fiona works on this problem: "There were 37 pigeons and 19 flew away. How many remained?" She starts the calculation by separating the tens and ones (30 – 10 = 20), next subtracts the 9 ones (20 – 9 = 11), and then becomes confused about what to do next. In order to figure it out, Fiona, at her teacher's suggestion, goes back to look again at the problem context: Did those pigeons leave or stay? Having posed that question, the girl decides that she needs to add back on the 7 from the 37 to get the answer, 18. What is the role of the story problem in helping Fiona figure out how to perform the calculation? What is it that Fiona understands about situations modeled by subtraction?

As a second example, we see Eleanor's class of third and fourth graders (case 18 in *Building a System of Tens*) perform the calculation for 4×27. As the children come up with various ways to reconfigure the numbers, what do they understand about the nature of multiplication that allows them to arrive at the answer, 108?

In another episode (case 22 in *Building a System of Tens*), when Betty and her sixth graders try to make sense of the conventional long-division algorithm to solve $72 \div 3$, they make up a story problem about three people sharing candy. How does the story problem serve them?

The cases in *Making Meaning for Operations* concentrate on such questions as these: What kinds of actions and situations are modeled by addition, subtraction, multiplication, and division? How do children, as they work with such situations, come to understand the operations? One seminar facilitator put it this way: "*Making Meaning for Operations* challenges our definition of *operation*. It brings operation out of a computation framework into a 'meaning' framework."

This casebook begins with a look at young children's counting strategies as they address problems that they will later solve by adding, subtracting, multiplying, or dividing. It then moves to an examination of the types of situations that are modeled by whole-number addition, subtraction, multiplication, and division. The latter part of the casebook revisits the operations in the context of rational numbers. Which of the children's ideas, issues, and generalizations need to be refined or revised when the problem situations involve rational numbers? For example, how are they to make sense of multiplying and dividing when the numbers being operated on—fractions—already imply division?

As in *Building a System of Tens*, the cases in this book were all written by teachers of grades K–7 describing events in their own classrooms. The teacher-authors were participating in a project in which they explored the ways students come to make meaning for operations; writing these cases was part of their process of inquiry.

Like the casebook for Part 1, this book concludes with a chapter called "Highlights of Related Research." This essay summarizes some recent research findings that touch on the issues explored in the 28 cases of *Making Meaning for Operations*.

C H A P T E R

1

Counting up, counting back, and counting by

As you read the following word problems, consider for a moment which of the operations—addition, subtraction, multiplication, or division—you would use to find the answer to each one.

There are 13 insects on the paper in front of us and 5 spiders behind my

back. What is the total number of insects and spiders?

We know that a bunny has 4 legs, so how many legs do 3 bunnies have?

There are 10 girls in our class and 8 are here today. How many girls are out today?

There are 12 blocks on the table, and 3 children want to play with the blocks. How many blocks can they each use?

We can easily identify the operations that would give us the answers: addition (13 + 5 = 18), subtraction (10 – 8 = 2), multiplication (4 × 3 = 12), and division (12 ÷ 3 = 4). But what is it that children must understand to solve these story problems? What happens when such problems are posed to children who have not yet learned the symbols for the operations (+, –, ×, ÷) and have not yet learned their arithmetic facts? How do children find answers to such problems when they haven't yet learned to add, subtract, multiply, or divide? This chapter presents seven cases that allow us to examine precisely these questions. As you read the following cases, take notes on these questions:

- While following the counting strategies that young children use to solve problems, and by pondering the confusions that arise for them, what do *we* learn about the operations?

- What do we learn about the ideas that children must put together in order for *them* to develop an understanding of the operations?

C A S E **1**

Insects and spiders and counting on

Dan

GRADE 1, SEPTEMBER

As part of our science study of insects and spiders, the children sorted small plastic models onto two large sheets of paper labeled *Insects* and *Spiders*. As they placed their models, they had to tell what attributes they were using to make their decisions. The following activity was an integration of math with this science study. After we sorted the models and confirmed that each was in the correct set, I asked, "How many

5

insects are there?"

The insects were positioned randomly on the sheet. I called on Mike. As he counted the insects, his finger jumped around from one to another, making it difficult to keep track of which ones he had counted and which he had missed. He ended up miscounting by 1, coming up with 14. Some children said they disagreed with his count.

I next asked Annie to count the insects. Although she didn't count them in an easily discernible order (e.g., left to right, or top to bottom, or by moving them as she counted), she was clearly able to keep track, since she did not recount or leave out any insects. She came up with the correct answer of 13.

I asked one more child, Renaldo, to count to see whether his answer would agree with either of the previous answers or would be completely different. He counted the insects in an organized way; as he said each number, he moved one item into a group of already counted insects. He came up with 13, just as Annie did.

I asked the group, "Why did we get different answers, 14 and 13?" Renaldo quickly replied that Mike had "counted too many." Nods from many of the children seemed to suggest agreement. I think he meant that Mike had counted some insect or insects more than once. Since the children seemed content with Renaldo's response, I assumed they agreed that 13 was the answer and did not pursue this question any further.

The children were quickly able to see that there were only 5 spiders on the other sheet. Since we had not counted the total number of insects and spiders, I decided to find out how the children would determine how many there were altogether if I removed the 5 spiders from view. How would they solve the problem? How would they represent items that were absent and keep them in the count? Would they start at 13 or at 1 to get the new count?

After I put the spiders behind my back I said, "If we know that there are 13 insects and that there are 5 spiders to be added, how many would there be altogether?"

Lindsey immediately raised her hand and answered 18. She explained that she thought of 13 insects in her head and counted on 5 more spiders in her head.

Then I called on Mike. He recounted the 13 insects very carefully, one by one (in contrast to his earlier somewhat careless, random counting), and then touched and counted 5 imaginary spiders with one hand while raising 5 fingers, one at a time, on his other hand. Like Lindsey, he also came up with 18.

Liliana took a different approach. She counted the 13 insects and then separated 5 from that group and counted them on from the 13, also ending up with 18.

I brought the 5 spiders into view and together we all counted the 13 insects and 5 spiders to confirm that there really were 18.

These three students seem to represent a developmental sequence that children may go through in becoming comfortable with adding quantities together. Liliana started from 1, counted the 13 visible insects, and then separated 5 from that group as a concrete way to keep track of the additional 5 that she was counting. Mike seemed to be less dependent on the concrete objects. He also started at 1 with the 13 insects but then counted the additional 5 by touching imaginary spiders with one hand while keeping track with 5 fingers on his other hand. He seemed to have internalized that there are a total of 5 fingers on one of his hands, since he did not count out the 5 fingers before he counted them on. It did not seem to be a problem for him that his fingers can be labeled "1, 2, 3, 4, 5" in one situation and "14, 15, 16, 17, 18" in another situation. Liliana and Mike either did not recognize or did not trust that the 13 previously counted insects would still be 13, or they could not comfortably start counting in the middle of the number sequence. Lindsey, on the other hand, clearly trusted that the new number included the original 13 and didn't feel a need to start counting from 1. She seemed able to visualize a group that she could label 13, plus 5 more individual spiders that she could easily count on in her head.

I wondered if the children had a sense of the commutative property of addition, and decided to investigate. Would they recognize that we would get the same answer whether we began with the 5 and added on 13, or began with 13 and added on 5?

I put the 13 insects behind my back, showed the children the 5 spiders, and asked how many there would be altogether if I were to add in the missing 13. Many of the children immediately said 18. I raised the question, "How do you know it is the same answer?" Although I can't recall a clear answer from anyone, they gave variations on knowing that there were still 13 insects and we had already counted 5 spiders. I asked if there was any way that we could count them all up by first using the 5 spiders that we could see. No one responded.

Were these children really understanding the commutative property for addition? Or was the answer easy for them because there were no new variables—that is, there were still *13 insects* and *5 spiders?* Even though I had changed the placement of each, the children may not have seen this as a different situation. Would they have said so quickly that the answer was still 18 if I had changed or eliminated a defining variable, for example, if the 13 and the 5 were all insects?

I tried a problem with different numbers to see how they would deal with adding on a missing number of items that was more than 10: "What if I told you there were 11 insects to add to the 5 spiders we already have in front of us?" Liliana counted the 5 spiders that she saw. Then, without counting out ten fingers beforehand, she continued counting on her fingers one at a time to 15, and said she needed 1 more to make 16.

I found it interesting that Liliana was not daunted by the fact that she had only ten fingers. She seemed to have internalized that all her fingers always make a group called "10" and 1 more finger makes another group called "11." In addition, Liliana seemed comfortable with the fact that her ten fingers could be called "1, 2, 3, 4, 5, 6, 7, 8, 9, 10" in one situation and "6, 7, 8, 9, 10, 11, 12, 13, 14, 15" in another.

To verify that the children understood the importance of one-to-one correspondence in counting, I added 11 insects to the group of 5 spiders. I counted the 5 carefully, and then I continued to count the extra 11 insects randomly until I was way into the 20s. Many of the children shouted "No!" and said I could only count each insect once. Renaldo recounted for the group, carefully moving and placing each one into a new group of already-counted insects. He got 16, confirming Liliana's answer.

Many of the children seem to understand the need for one-to-one correspondence and for only counting each item one time so that you get a specific answer that is repeatable. Many may have some sense of the commutative property for addition, but I cannot be sure of this without further investigation. Some of them clearly understand that a group of items has a constant value even when another group is added to them, and that it is not necessary to start over from 1 when adding the new items on one by one; others do not have this awareness or trust yet. Some interesting questions come up: When do children move from merely counting to actually understanding *addition?* Is it when they can count on from a number, rather than having to start again from 1? Or can children who have to start at 1 every time still understand that they are adding and not just counting?

Mr. McIntosh's apples

Emma

KINDERGARTEN, OCTOBER

I posed the following question to my kindergarten class:

> **?** Mr. McIntosh had 3 apples. His son Allan picked 6 more apples from their apple tree and gave them to his father. How many apples does Mr. McIntosh have all together?

125

I explained to the children that many people do lots of thinking to help them solve a problem. I told them that throughout the year, I would be bringing them problems that they could help me with.

I read the story problem to them twice. Then I asked, "What do you think? Would anyone like to give a prediction, a guess, a thought?" Everyone in the class of 23 wanted to make a prediction. Here are just a few of their responses:

130

MANUEL: 9. I added.

ANDRE: 9. Because my brain told me to say it.

JOEY: 9. When you take 3 and 6, you make them go to another number, 9. [*He then counted*]: 6 [*pause*] . . . 7, 8, 9.

135

STEFANIE: It's 9. I added.

VERONICA: 150. There are many, many of them.

MARTINA: 5. We are five years old.

Then I told them that some people use counters when solving problems with numbers, and asked "Would you like to try?" I was surprised at their enthusiastic response; they were eager to try this. I brought out a tub of Unifix® cubes with different-sized plastic containers.

140

Each container is sized to hold a specific number of cubes and is labeled at the end with the corresponding numeral.* 145

Manuel selected the number-3 and number-6 containers. He filled them with cubes, then took out each group of cubes to connect them in a stack. As he connected the cubes, he counted them. Then he connected the 3-cube and 6-cube stacks together into a single stack. He counted, recounted, and then stated, "I added them together. It makes 9." 150

Andre put 3 cubes together in one stack and 6 cubes together in another. He connected the two stacks, counted all the cubes, and stated, "I have 9."

Joey started with 9 cubes, which he stacked. Then he broke that stack apart into a stack of 3 and a stack of 6. Joey reported, "If you take 6 and 3, that makes 9." As he spoke, he reconnected the two, making one whole 155 stack of 9.

Stefanie put 9 cubes together, saying, "3 + 3 + 3 make 9." As she spoke she pointed to each group of 3 cubes.

Veronica put 34 cubes together and started counting them. Then she said, "There's 34. I put lots of them together and that's how I made them 160 tall." From this response and others I have heard from Veronica, I can see that she is fascinated with large numbers, and I sense the power that "many, many of them" has for her. The entire time she was working, she used her voice, hands, and body to express the largeness of her number— as she has on other occasions. I would like to meet Veronica at this level 165 of thinking by doing other problem solving with both large and small numbers, making observations and comparisons of them, helping her with this concept of "how many."

Martina placed 4 cubes in a number-8 plastic container. She then removed the stack of 4 cubes, placed a number-8 plastic lid on top, and 170 held the stack beside the the number-8 plastic container, stating, "Look. It matches!" She was comparing the two numerals on the plastic lid and the plastic container, both 8. Even though she didn't count the correct number of cubes to fill the number-8 container, she was showing her ability to recognize the numeral 8. She then took the number-10 container 175 and filled it with cubes. She connected these cubes to the stack of 4, saying, "It's nice and tall."

---

*These containers are the Unifix 1–10 Value Boats, or trays that hold from one to ten cubes in a single stack. The "plastic lid" referred to later in this case is one of the Unifix Number Indicators, each shaped like a little triangular roof and labeled on both sides with a numeral, to be placed on top of a cube or stack of cubes.

Emma

It fascinated me to see that one problem-solving question revealed so much of the processing and thinking going on in my class. I was able to assess those children who understood the concept of addition and consider *how* they understood it. Often we do not look deeper into the "wrong answer" responses. By looking at the children's thinking, I am able to assess the stage they are at and to plan future learning experiences for them.

180

C A S E 3

Going up and down with numbers

KINDERGARTEN, MARCH

As we start each day in kindergarten, we assemble at the rug area for our opening meeting. One of the things we discuss is the number of children in school. This morning, as usual, we counted the number of boys, which today totaled 9, and then the number of girls, which totaled 8. I wrote on the chalkboard:

185

9 boys

190

8 girls

I then asked, "How many boys are out today?"

Natalie raised her hand and answered, "When all the boys are here, we have 10 boys, so today we have 9 boys, so 1 boy is out."

"How many girls are out today?"

195

Peter raised his hand and said, "It's 2." He knew that there were 10 girls in the class when all were present.

I asked, "How did you figure it out?"

Peter replied, "8 and 1 and . . . " He seemed to be stuck in his thinking. I feel he did figure it out correctly but then had trouble explaining.

200

I then asked, "Can someone else tell me how many girls are out today?"

Denisha's hand went up. She said, "It's 2, because 8 is 2 numbers down from 10."

"What does that mean?" I asked Denisha.   205

"When all the girls are here, it's 10," she told us. "You go down from 10 by 1, that's 9, and down 1 more, that's 8, so that's 2."

We usually count around the circle to find the total number in class for the day. I decided instead to see if the children could come up with the total just by looking at the numbers.   210

9 boys

8 girls

"How many kids here today?" I asked.

Daniel answered, "17."

I said, "Daniel, if you look at the numbers of boys and girls, can you   215
tell me how you got 17?" He didn't reply. I think that Daniel counted around the circle and didn't want to tell me that.

Rachelle offered, "8 and 9 makes a 1 and a 7." When I asked Rachelle how she knew that, she answered, "I counted in my mind."

"How did you count in your mind? Say it out loud."   220

She began, "1, 2, 3, 4, 5, 6, 7, 8, 9 . . . " But she didn't go on. She wasn't using her fingers, so I'm not sure how she was going to explain the answer.

"Did anyone else figure it out in a different way?" I wondered.

Tamara's hand went up and she said, "It's 17, 8 and 9. If you took 1   225
away from the 9 it becomes an 8, and 8 and 8 makes 16, so you put the 9 back. You go up one more from 8, you make a 9 and you have the 8, you get 17. You're going one more higher than 16."

I was amazed at how several of the children could see the relationship that numbers have to each other. They used the phrase "going up or   230
down" to describe this. Tamara "went down" one from the 9 to make 8. It seemed easier for her to add 8 and 8, yet she knew that 9 was 1 more than 8 so the 16 had to "go up" by one. I feel that Peter was thinking about "going up" when he said 8 and 1, but couldn't say the 1 more to make 10. Denisha described "going down" from 10 by 1, and by 1 again to get 8.   235
She then knew 2 girls were absent. Being able to go up and down with numbers seems to be a key to understanding number differences.

Complexities of counting backwards

Denise

GRADE 2, OCTOBER

I've been interested for the past year in the ways second graders come to understand addition, subtraction, and regrouping. I've watched children invent methods that reflect a tremendous amount of what I termed "sophistication" and flexibility in how they think about numbers. Among the "least sophisticated" methods for subtracting that I identified were kids counting backwards on their fingers, or collecting an amount of counters, say 22, for example, and then taking away 5.

I am also interested in seeing how kids move toward increasingly sophisticated and flexible thinking about number. In the first couple of weeks of school, I actively watched for examples that would help me begin to illuminate something (who knows just what?) about number sense. What I found was a surprise. I'm very interested in hearing if anyone is similarly puzzled, grabbed, or surprised by this event!

The activity we were working on is called "Enough for the Class" (from *Mathematical Thinking at Grade 2,* in the curriculum *Investigations in Number, Data, and Space,* © 1998 by Dale Seymour Publications). I show my class a bag of cubes and tell them we need to figure out if there are enough cubes in the bag for everyone in our class to take one. If there are too many or too few, *how many* too many or too few are there?

As a class we counted the cubes in the bag and found that there were 32. We had 25 students in our class that day.

I witnessed students solving this problem in a variety of ways. Some solved it by adding on their fingers from 25 to 32 and getting 7. Others solved it by counting backwards from 32 until they got to 25. Others saw that by adding 5 to 25 they got to 30 quickly, and then added 2 more to the 5. Some solved it with cubes stacked to a length of 32, taking off cubes until there were 25.

Susan counted backwards and recorded her method on her paper like this: 32 I I I I I I 25. She got 6 for her answer.

The next day when we discussed different students' methods, there was general agreement that 7 was the answer. I called on Susan, hoping she'd talk about her method. Instead, she used a strip of 32 cubes that a classmate had just used. She took off 7 cubes one by one and indeed got 25. (I was a little disappointed; I had hoped she would bring her method to the class.) Then her face looked puzzled and she said, "But I remember yesterday I got 6."

I said, "But today you got 7. Hmm. How could that be?"

Susan repeated her process with 32 cubes, recounting to be sure there were really 32 cubes in her strip and then carefully taking off 7 and recounting those remaining 25 cubes again. She was very puzzled.

Other students restated their process that gave them the answer 7, and Susan was still puzzled. I asked her to look again at her paper and reminded her, "Didn't you count backwards, Susan?"

Susan looked at her work from the previous day more closely. "Oh yes, I did."

I drew on the board what Susan had drawn yesterday, 32 | | | | | | 25, and said, "This is what Susan drew. There's the 6."

Some children said, "Yeah, there's 6."

This was a genuine confusion for a few minutes as students buzzed about how they had got 7, but here was Susan getting 6 one way and 7 another.

In a few seconds Clara said, "Well, Susan has to take away either the 32 or the 25 in order to get 7."

I said, "Right, but why?"

Several other children offered up how and why 7 was in fact the answer. They pointed out that with 32 cubes, you are taking away the 32nd cube, the 31st cube, the 30th cube, the 29th, the 28th, the 27th, and the 26th cube, and then you are left with 25 cubes.

25 cubes	7	6	5	4	3	2	1
	26	27	28	29	30	31	32

But when you count backwards on your fingers or out loud, you start at 32 and don't count 1 until you get to 31, then 2 is at 30, 3 is at 29, 4 is at 28, 5 is at 27, 6 is at 26, and when you count back the 7th time, you get to 25.

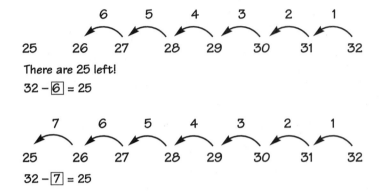

There are 25 left!

$32 - \boxed{6} = 25$

$32 - \boxed{7} = 25$

Drawing these diagrams myself much later highlighted the complexities in a method I had always assumed was "less sophisticated." Indeed, this counting backwards does seem simple at first glance. But, if I didn't know already that 32 take away 7 is 25, how would I construct and make sense of the difference between these two ways of thinking? In my quest to investigate number sense and to identify how children develop it, this moment really sits with me still.

In fact, this issue came up several weeks later when we were considering how many kids are here in class if 4 of them are absent. Ricky reasoned similarly to Susan's first assertion in my earlier example, that 26 . . . 25 (1) . . . 24 (2) . . . 23 (3) . . . 22 (4), and there's 21 left. So there must be 21 kids here.

Many children spoke up quickly and heatedly, insisting that they knew 22 plus 4 is 26, so if there are 4 kids *not* here, there must be 22 here. Others clamored that Ricky had to take away the 26 first, or that he got to 22 as he took away the 4th kid. Many of my students are quite convinced and clear about how they would take 4 away from 26. Ricky and Susan have simply piqued my interest about how they will *become* convinced, now that I consider some of the complexities of what might or might not happen in their construct.

300

305

310

315

Counting days and counting by

KINDERGARTEN, DECEMBER

Each morning as part of our daily meeting, my class charts the number of days we have been in school. I record the new number for each day in a two-inch square on a 10-by-18 grid. In addition, in an attempt to make this more concrete for kindergarten students, this year I have the calendar helper snap another Unifix cube onto a collection sitting on the chalkboard ledge. We started this routine the first day of school, and the "train" (as my students refer to the collection of cubes) has grown by one each day. We often count the train to ensure that it matches the number on our chart and correct any errors as needed. After about the 20th day, the train became too cumbersome to hold. It often fell apart in chunks as we picked it up, thus making it more difficult for everyone to see and count.

The situation provided a context for me to pose the following question to my kindergarten students: "Is there any other way we can organize our train so that it will be easier to count the cubes?"

The first time I asked this question, there wasn't any response, so I let it go. A few days later, the train fell apart again as one child tried to count the cubes. I posed my question again, and this time the responses included, "We could make a pile," and "We could make it a pattern." As the discussion continued, the class decided that a pile would be too hard to store, and no one could propose a pattern that could help us. Again, I let it go.

On the 57th day of school, the same situation arose again. This time, responses to my question were very different.

MARIKA: We could break it in threes.

NEERA: Maybe fives, sixes, sevens, or eights.

DWIGHT: I think ten, eleven, or three, or five.

Carolyn

RYAN: How about twenty?

ALLEGRA: Just don't pick it up.

STEVEN: Nineteens.

SHELLEY: One hundreds.

ETHAN: We could use it for adding.

I was delighted by the progress of this ongoing investigation. I suggested that maybe in small groups, children could try out their ideas. The first takers were Marika, Justin, Shelley, and Ethan.

TEACHER: How do you think we should begin?

SHELLEY: Just leave them down where it is and count it without squashing it.

Marika and Shelley quickly began counting the cubes. They chimed along together, touching each cube until about 13, when Marika pulled back a bit. Shelley continued with the count, touching each cube until 39. She skipped saying the 40s altogether and went from 39 to 50. After a while, she began to repeat numbers and finally ended up saying "57."

TEACHER: Is that how many we should have?

All four kids said yes. No one seemed to notice that Shelley had omitted numbers and had miscounted along the way. I bit my tongue as they all seemed to believe that since she said 57 on the last cube as she touched it, that 57 was, indeed, the number she counted.

JUSTIN: But I want to try.

Justin began counting and started and stopped several times before speaking.

JUSTIN: She's distracting me.

We spoke briefly about how hard it is to count and that it would be polite if everyone could count silently while Justin gave it a try. He proceeded to count and touched each cube, one at a time, as he counted from 1 to 29.

16	Making Meaning for Operations

JUSTIN: What comes after 29?

SHELLEY: 30.

Justin continued his count until 39.

JUSTIN: What comes next?

SHELLEY: 50.

This was the same place Shelley started omitting numbers when she was counting the cubes. Again, I decided not to intervene. Justin continued touching each cube carefully, saying "50, 51, 52, 53, 54, 55, 56, 57, 58, 59, 60, 61, 62, 63, 64, 65, 66, 67." Since he omitted the 40s, this answer made sense to me, but the kids were confused.

SHELLEY: How can it be 67? I got 57.

MARIKA: The number of days is 57.

Marika got up and went over to our chart to check her thinking. All along, Ethan had been sitting patiently.

ETHAN: I have another idea. I split it in 5s, but I got one more
            at the end.

TEACHER: What do you mean?

ETHAN: I'll show you.

Ethan pulled the train of cubes closer to himself and began counting, snapping off a group of 5 cubes. He did this a few times, and then Shelley and Marika began counting off 5 cubes, putting them into stacks of 5 as Ethan did. At one point, Marika had a stack of 6 cubes.

ETHAN: Marika, just break off that blue one; then it will be 5.

This continued until there were 11 stacks of 5 sitting on the table. In his hand, Ethan held 2 cubes.

ETHAN: How can this be? I got 2 more at the end.

A long pause followed. Then he had an idea. Ethan arranged the 11 stacks in front of him:

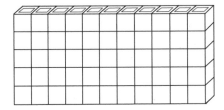

He continued to hold 2 cubes in his hand.

ETHAN: I guess it *is* 2 left.

TEACHER: What makes you sure now?

ETHAN: 'Cause I know these all have 5, and there are 2 left over here. [*He places the two remaining cubes on the table next to the stacks.*]

TEACHER: So how many are there?

JUSTIN: I don't know.

ETHAN: 57.

SHELLEY: 57.

MARIKA: It has to be 57. That's how many days we've been in school.

Working with these children for no more than 15 minutes yielded a lot of powerful experiences. On one level, we were all reminded that counting is difficult work. We can easily become distracted, as Justin reminds us. Holding onto the right number seems to be something that these children are wrestling with. As the configuration changed, Justin no longer saw the 57. On the other hand, Marika and Shelley were sure it was 57 all along. "It has to be," Marika tells us. And yet, with all of Marika's confidence in 57 as the number of days, she never actually counted all 57 cubes herself.

Where Marika is still working on one-to-one correspondence, and Shelley and Justin have shown us that remembering the number names is an important aspect of counting that young children need to work on,

Ethan gives us a glimpse of the world to come. His idea of breaking the 57 into groups of 5 was very impressive to me. With his configuration on the table, later I asked Ethan if he could count the cubes for me.

ETHAN: I can only do it a little. I know 5, 10, but I don't know what comes next.

TEACHER: How could you figure this out?

ETHAN: I guess I could count. 5, 10, 1, 2, 3, 4, 5. No, I mean, 11, 12, 13, 14, 15. That's 15. [*He moves three of the stacks of 5 over to one side.*]

Ethan continued to count by ones from 16 to 55. As he touched each cube in the stack of 5, he moved it over into another pile. Finally, he came to the last 2 cubes.

ETHAN: 56, 57. See, it has to be 57!

Yes, I thought to myself. I guess it does!

C A S E   6

Bunnies and eggs

Bella

KINDERGARTEN, APRIL

Since Easter was coming up, I decided to do some problems about bunny rabbits. After a discussion on the number of legs one bunny rabbit has, I drew a picture of a bunny on the chalkboard and asked the children to solve the following problem:

? If one bunny has 4 legs, how many legs would 3 bunnies have?

I told them that they could use any manipulative they wished to solve the problem. I was quite interested in the various representations they came up with.

Bella

KINDERGARTEN, APRIL

Jason built his rabbits from colored wooden blocks; each rabbit had a head, a body, and four legs. He came over to me and said, "Mrs. Waters, I got 12 legs." I asked him how he got the answer, and he told me he counted them. I asked him to draw me a picture of what he had done. Figure 1 shows his drawing.

Rashad used the large plastic keys we keep in a bucket in the room. He placed one key horizontally for each body, four keys perpendicular to it for the legs, and made three of these arrangements (see Figure 2).

I asked, "How many legs did you get?" and Rashad told me 12. When I asked him to show me how he got 12, he counted, pointing to each "leg" in turn. I was surprised that he didn't get confused about which keys were legs and which represented the body.

Carlita also used keys to represent the problem. First she made one row of four keys and told me that she had one rabbit. I asked her where the other rabbits were, and she said she would make them. I watched her build a second row of four keys, and then a third row (see Figure 3).

"See, I have 3 rabbits."

"How many legs are there in all?" I asked.

Carlita counted her keys: "Twelve."

Figure 1. Jason's drawing of three bunnies, four legs each.

Figure 2. Rashad's arrangement of keys, another way of representing three bunnies.

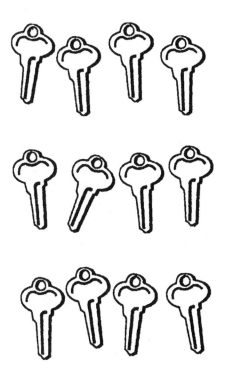

Figure 3. Carlita's arrangement of keys, showing four legs for each of three rabbits.

Bella

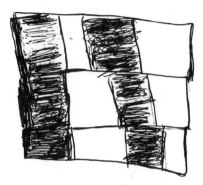

Figure 4. Kenya's picture of cubes representing three four-legged bunnies.

Kenya used Unifix cubes, snapping together three groups of orange and white cubes in an a-b-a-b pattern. She counted them all together to get her answer and made a picture of what she had done (see Figure 4).

When I got to Flora, she had a row of 12 rocks in front of her (see Figure 5).

"How many legs did you get?"

"I got 12."

"Can you tell me how you did it?"

"I counted one bunny first; then I counted the next bunny's; then I counted the next bunny."

"So how did you know how many legs there were in all?"

"I counted all of them."

Mark, Quincy, and Jerome were busy building their rabbits out of Legos®. They built great looking rabbits with four legs, but time ran out before they could solve the problem.

The children were all so engaged in solving the problem that, even when I announced lunch time, they didn't want to leave. There was no one in the group who was not working on the problem.

Figure 5. Flora's rocks, representing the 12 legs on three bunnies.

Making Meaning for Operations

Bella

The children enjoyed being given the problem to solve, though I was aware that some of them still have difficulty counting even those small numbers. Besides the children whose representations I have described here, there were some who were not able to figure out the total.

Several days later, I decided to give a similar problem; this time I wanted to see what was going on with the children who had difficulty.

 I made 3 Easter baskets for my friends. In each basket, I put 3 eggs. How many eggs were there in all?

Again, I told the children they could use whatever manipulatives they might choose.

Jenna used the Unifix cubes. First she made a unit of 3 cubes and brought them over to show me. I asked her what she had, and she said that she had one basket.

"Where are the other baskets?" I asked.

"I haven't made them yet," she said, heading back to the table. Soon she was back again, this time with two units of 3.

"How many baskets do you have now?"

"Two."

"How many baskets did I say were needed?"

"Three."

"Where are they?"

Jenna went off again and returned with the third unit of 3. "How many eggs do you have?" I asked.

"I don't know. I haven't counted them yet." She proceeded to count all the cubes and soon arrived at her answer: 9 eggs.

Jenna really surprised me with her understanding of the problem. She very rarely participates in an activity in a way that helps me understand what she really knows. Today I was impressed.

Junior also worked with Unifix cubes. He had 3 orange ones, 3 white, and 3 yellow.

"What do you have?" I asked.

"Three baskets."

"How many eggs are in each basket?"

"Three."

"How many eggs do you have in all?"

"Three."

Junior showed me how he counted: Each unit of 3 was "one" to him. I took one unit and broke it apart. He counted them, "1, 2, 3," and agreed

485

490

495

500

505

510

515

520

that they represented 3 eggs. I put them back together with the other two units of 3 and asked him how many eggs were there. Again he said, "Three." I tried several ways to help him see that I wanted him to count the individual cubes, but it didn't help. He was unable to see the difference or sameness between cubes once they became a single unit of 3.

Several of the children had no difficulty with this problem, so for them I posed an extension:

 If I added 1 more egg to each basket, how many eggs would there be?

When I gave the second problem to Mark and Quincy, they both went away and soon returned with an answer. Mark explained, "I put 3 more on the 3 baskets. One more egg to 3 baskets, and that makes 12." Quincy had the same answer, but when I asked him how he got it, he said, "Mark told me."

Jason presented me with three groups of 3 Unifix cubes to demonstrate his answer of 9 to the first problem. When I asked him to solve the second problem, he added only a single cube and said there were 10. I repeated the question at least twice to see if he could figure out what was wrong with his answer and how he could fix it, but he did not change his answer.

Rashad had no problem figuring out the first problem, using an arrangement of three rows of 3 keys each. When I gave him the second problem, he added 1 key to each group and said there were 12 eggs. Seeing how easily he arrived at the answer, I decided to challenge him with another extension:

 I have another friend, and I would also like to give this friend an Easter basket with the same number of eggs. How many eggs would there be in all?

"I added one more basket," he said. "Four baskets with 4 eggs: 16." Only after he gave an answer did he count the added keys. "See, I was right!" Rashad, it seems, has an ability to think about numbers at a level beyond his age.

As usual, I was unable to get around to all the children, but I learned more about what my class knows and how they handle problems. A couple of years ago, I wouldn't have attempted *any* of this kind of mathematics with children of this age. I would have thought that this is too difficult for them. How wrong I would have been!

Thinking about division

Christina

KINDERGARTEN, OCTOBER

Recently I have been thinking about how kindergarten students might go about solving a division problem. Learning to share is a big focus of the social/emotional aspect of a kindergarten program, but I hadn't ever thought about the complex mathematical thinking that dividing a set of objects requires of five- and six-year-olds. Often when I observe children at play, when sharing materials is required, they simply grab what they need and don't question the equity of the quantity unless another child thinks that he or she did not get a fair share. This conflict is usually resolved by children voicing what they see as an injustice and then redistributing items in a way that seems more fair. More often than not, this does not entail any actual counting, but rather eyeballing or estimating quantities.

A few days ago I decided to see what my students would do with a sharing or division problem that specifically asked them to think about equal quantities. I posed the following question:

? There are 12 blocks on the table. Three children want to play with the blocks. How many blocks can they each use?

Initially I suggested that the children use Unifix cubes to help solve the problem. Each child I watched took out 12 cubes and either snapped them together in a train or piled them up as they counted. Several children showed some confusion in counting a set of 12 cubes. Whenever I noticed any confusion with counting (one-to-one correspondence), I asked that child to recount his or her set for me. Most children noticed their own errors and were able to adjust their set. If they were not, then I suggested we count together.

When each child had a set of 12 cubes, I restated the problem. I was particularly intrigued by the immediate responses of two children. The ideas came out so quickly, they seemed almost to be gut-level responses.

THOMAS: You can't do that! Three? No way! 'Cause 6 plus 6 is 12. You can't have 3.

EMILIO: That's easy, it's 4. See, 1, 2, 3, 4 . . . 1, 2, 3, 4 . . . 1, 2, 3, 4. 590

With two quick snaps, Emilio had broken his train of 12 cubes into three equal groups of 4 cubes each and counted off each section aloud. It's as if he just saw the solution and didn't even have to think about it.

As I observed more children, I noticed that two different methods were emerging. Some children broke off equal sets of cubes, and others 595 broke off cubes one at a time and put them into equal piles. I never saw a child who did not have equal quantities in each group. And then I noticed something that really surprised me.

When I approached Desiree, she had her train of 12 cubes in her hand.

TEACHER: Do you have 12 cubes? 600

DESIREE: Yes!

TEACHER: What happens if 3 people want to share the 12 cubes?

DESIREE: I think it's 12.

TEACHER: What do you mean?

Desiree snapped off a set of 3 cubes and put it on the table. Then she 605 repeated this action three more times until she had four groups of 3 cubes on the table.

DESIREE: See, 3 people, so I made threes.

TEACHER: What do mean, you made threes?

DESIREE: I made 3 in each one. 610

TEACHER: So you have 3 cubes in each one. How many kids can use these blocks?

DESIREE: Three. No, four. Wait a minute . . .

Desiree reassembled her original train of 12 cubes and broke them apart again. This time she broke them off one at a time and said, "One for 615 you, one for me, and one for Hannah," as she created three piles with 4 cubes in each. Next she reconnected each set of 4 cubes to show three equal sets.

DESIREE: It's now 4.

TEACHER: What do you mean, it's now 4?   620

DESIREE: You get 4 and so do I.

TEACHER: [*Pointing to the third set*] Who gets these?

DESIREE: Hannah does.

TEACHER: Do we all get the same amount?

DESIREE: Yes.   625

I watched as several children set themselves up in a similar situation. They seemed to be drawn more to the number *in the set* and operated on that first, as opposed to the number of sets. I'm not sure what this tells me, but I thought it was really interesting that I noticed several children with the same situation. The problem asked them to share the 12 blocks among 3 children, but somehow this got played out as 3 cubes in each set. Most of the children were able to sort this out over time, but not Tony. He also started by snapping together a train of 12 cubes. When I approached him about the problem, he unsnapped 3 at a time, as Desiree had, and netted four sets of 3.   630   635

TEACHER: Can you tell me about your work?

TONY: See, 3 and 3 and 3 and 3 make 12.

TEACHER: How many kids are going to play with these blocks?

TONY: Three.

TEACHER: But I see four piles.   640

TONY: OK, nobody gets these. [*He takes away one set.*]

TEACHER: How many blocks do you have now?

TONY: [*Touching each block and counting to himself*] Nine.

TEACHER: But you're supposed to have 12.

Tony studied the situation for a long time. He would put back the fourth set, then take it away again. At one point he suggested to me that a fourth person could play, but I reminded him that only 3 kids could play.   645

He just seemed caught between four sets of 3 and three sets of 3. At no point did he ever show that he could break the fourth set apart and redistribute the 3 elements among the three established sets. It was really fascinating to watch him go back and forth. I wonder what this shows about the interrelatedness of *number of groups* and *numbers in a group?*

I thought a lot about this work and how similarly children seemed to go about solving the problem. I noticed that more kids broke the trains apart to make sets, rather than dealing the cubes out one at a time, and I wondered if it was because of the materials. Two children were absent the day we did this problem, so when they returned, I decided to give them a different type of material—some stones we have in the class. I also wanted to see what would happen if I changed the problem a little. When I worked with Madeline and Nora, I asked them first to solve the problem for 2 children instead of 3.

When Madeline started working, she had difficulty counting out a set of 12 stones. First she counted to 12, but actually had 10. Next, she counted to 10 and then put 4 more out, saying "12." Finally, we counted them together; she got 14, and decided to put 2 away. On her final count she got 12.

TEACHER: Do you have 12 stones?

MADELINE: Yes.

TEACHER: How many stones can each child have if there are 2 children playing?

MADELINE: Twelve? [*pause*] . . . 3? [*pause*] . . . 2?

Madeline seemed to be guessing.

TEACHER: Can you show me?

Madeline moved 2 stones from her pile of 12, and then another 2 stones, and then another. She continued until she had 6 piles, each with 2 stones.

TEACHER: How many children are going to play with the stones?

MADELINE: Two.

TEACHER: Can you show me the stones they are each going to use?

Madeline pushed 2 stones toward me and 2 stones toward herself.

MADELINE: Two for you and 2 for me.

TEACHER: What are you going to do with the other stones?

Madeline pushed 2 more stones toward me and added 2 to her pile. Then she did the same thing a second time.

MADELINE: Two more for you, 2 more for me, 2 more for you, 2 more for me.

TEACHER: How many stones do we each get?

MADELINE: [*After counting her set and then mine*] Six.

TEACHER: Now what happens if 3 kids want to share the 12 stones?

This time Madeline pulled all the stones back into one pile and doled them out one at a time, creating 3 equal sets with 4 in each, determining that each kid gets 4 stones.

Nora was the last student I observed. What a treat! I first noticed that Nora had lined her 12 stones in a neat row.

TEACHER: How can 2 children share these 12 stones?

NORA: We would each have 6.

TEACHER: How do you know for sure?

NORA: I took a few apart. [*She had moved 6 stones to one side.*] I noticed 6 and 6 make 12. I also saw 3 and 3 make 6.

TEACHER: Now what if 3 kids want to share the 12 stones?

Nora moved her stones into four groups of 3.

TEACHER: Tell me your thinking.

Before she spoke, she rearranged the stones to show three groups of 4 by taking one group of 3 and sharing the stones equally among her other sets.

TEACHER: Why did you change?

NORA: We could give them each 4. I divided them all into threes, so I saw 3 left, so I put one with one batch of 3, and one with another batch of 3, and one with the last batch of 3.

TEACHER: What would happen if 4 kids wanted to play?

NORA: This would be easy. [*She quickly moves her stones to show 4 sets of 3.*] We would have 4 threes. Everybody would have 3.   710

Needless to say, I was highly impressed with Nora's ability to express her thinking and show her solutions. But I was equally impressed with the way all the children explored the idea of division. They all seemed to understand something about equal numbers in a set and about how to   715
establish sets. I am particularly intrigued with what happens as they begin to sort out the difference between numbers in a set and number of sets. I have never formally presented a division problem to my kindergarten students before, but I will not hesitate to do it again in the future. It was fascinating to watch, listen, and learn.   720

C H A P T E R

2

Addition and subtraction as models

The children we read about in chapter 1 could solve a variety of problems through counting. In chapter 2 many of the children have developed more sophisticated understandings of operations. As we examine the arithmetic these children use to represent problems posed to them, more questions arise. One set of questions involves mathematical issues for ourselves:

- What does it mean to model a situation with an arithmetic sentence? In what ways does the arithmetic match the situation?

- Can a single situation be modeled by different number sentences?

- Can a single operation model different kinds of actions?

A second set of questions involves the children's processes of putting ideas together:

- In these samples from grades 1–3, what can we observe about the ways in which children's ideas develop?

- What appear to be some of the difficulties children face as they learn about addition and subtraction?

C A S E **8**

Red, blue, and yellow paint

Jane

GRADES 2 AND 3, OCTOBER

The second- and third-grade students in the multi-age class were just beginning to settle into the routine of their class. The classroom teacher and I had divided the 24 students into two equal groups: those who could add and subtract with regrouping went with their teacher, and those who couldn't stayed with me, their principal. My group consisted of four third graders and eight second graders. I decided to present a lesson on drawing pictures to solve problems.

I passed out large sheets of white paper and crayons. "I'm going to read you a problem," I said, "and I want you to draw a picture to show how you would solve it." I read this problem:

> **?** The class is going to make a large mural. They get 4 containers of red paint, 3 containers of blue paint, and 1 container of yellow paint. How many containers of paint did they get in all?

"Wait, how many containers of red paint?"
"How many blue?"
"How many yellow?"

I reread the problem, and the students began to work. As I walked around the room to see what they were doing, I noticed that, in typical fashion, some of the students were very carefully drawing their containers; others were making only circles to represent the containers. All of them were connecting their pictures to the problem.

Next, I asked the students to write a number sentence that would show how to solve the problem. The students went to work. Again, I walked around the room and noticed that students were writing several different sentences. I wondered if they would see any differences among their number sentences, and if they did, how they would explain them.

When we came together as a whole group, I asked for volunteers to show their number sentences. Josh's hand went up first. I smiled. Josh worked with me last year when I was a classroom teacher, and he has made so much progress. Last year at this time, he would never have raised his hand first.

Josh wrote his number sentence on the board:

$$4 + 3 + 1 = 8$$

I asked him to explain why he wrote the problem that way. "Well, there were 4 red containers—that's the 4, and 3 blue containers, and 1 yellow container. So 8 paints in all."

Josh's classmates shared their number sentences: $1 + 3 + 4 = 8$, $4 + 1 + 3 = 8$, and other permutations of the three addends. The order seemed to depend on either how the students had drawn their pictures, or the order they had heard when I repeated the problem. "Do all these numbers make sense for this problem?" I asked. Lance started to shake his head no, then stopped and looked puzzled.

"It depends on which ones they got first," Charlene said, and I asked her what she meant. "They went to get the red first so it comes first, then the blue, then the yellow."

"I thought she got them all at the same time," said Jacinta.

"That doesn't matter; it's just how many they have in all," Malia said. When I questioned her further, she said, "If she gets red, blue, then yellow, she has 8, and if she gets blue, then yellow, then red, she still has 8."

"What if they mixed the paints?" Clarissa asked. The group discussed this for a while, but decided that the paints wouldn't be mixed for the mural.

Then Shiro shared his number sentence, $4 + 4 = 8$. I asked if Shiro's

number sentence matched the problem. The group had different
responses. Some said yes, his number sentence did match the problem
because he had 8 containers in all. Others said no, because they couldn't
see the various colors of paint. "It's like he mixed the blue and yellow,"
Clarissa said. "That's what it would look like."

"But that's not the same problem," Charlene objected. "The problem
didn't say they were mixed."

55

60

CASE 9

Enough for the class

Melinda

GRADE 2, OCTOBER

My second graders have had several opportunities to work on what we
have come to call "Enough for the Class" problems. The format of the
problems is this:

> **?** There are X objects in a bag. Are there enough for every kid
> in the class to take one? If yes, how many would be left in the
> bag? If no, how many more are needed?

65

There are 26 students in my class, and the number of objects in the bag
has ranged from 15 to 55. I have always had an actual bag of objects
when we did these problems.

Some interesting issues have come up. For the first problem we tried,
there were 38 cubes in the bag. We counted the cubes by ones at the
meeting area. There was resounding consensus that there were enough
cubes for every child to take one, and that there would be some left over.
The question of how many were left over, which I wanted them to solve
with a partner or independently, was much more difficult for several of
the children. These children did not find a way into the problem during
that first math period. Their confusion was increased exponentially by my
insistence that they *show their thinking* on paper.

70

75

Melinda

GRADE 2, OCTOBER

I wondered if using smaller numbers would help these students to understand the structure of the problem. The next day I presented them with this example:

> **?** There are 9 pieces of candy in a bag. There are 5 children. Are there enough pieces of candy for each child to take one? How many will be left in the bag?

Many hands flew up right away. A few children called out "Four!" Many more hands went up after a moment or two. No one disagreed with the answer of 4, and several children described how they figured it out. We modeled the problem with cubes, lines, pictures of candy, and check marks. Children talked about $5 + 4 = 9$ and $9 - 5 = 4$. In contrast to the previous day, many children now participated in the discussion, and the majority seemed to be following what we were talking about. We also talked about how they might show their thinking for the various methods used to solve the problem, which is a topic in itself.

During the next several math times, the children had a choice of a number of activities, one of which was "Enough for the Class." For that choice, I set out several bags of objects. When I went to watch Ebony at work, she asked me again what she was supposed to do. I indicated the bag of 41 pencils she had chosen and asked, "Do you think there are enough pencils in here for everyone in the class to have one?" When the girl indicated yes, I asked her, "How could you find out for sure?"

"Count," Ebony suggested. I nodded, and she counted the pencils by ones. I asked if there would be enough for the class (she said yes), and how she might figure out how many would be left over. She said she could take out 26 pencils. She did so, and counted the remainder. Ebony wrote $41 - 26 = 15$ on her paper. She said she "got it," so I moved on.

When I returned later, Ebony had been joined at the activity by a couple of other children. Ebony continued to work with other bags of objects in a way similar to her first approach, and she explained the activity to newcomers. I was very interested to see several children solving the problems without ever counting or figuring out the total number of objects in the bag. Annamarie would empty the bag onto the table, separate out 26 objects, and then count the rest. She wrote down the remainder, and was done. She worked almost automatically, giving the impression of going through prescribed steps for me as I watched. Nonetheless, Annamarie could show which pile was, for example, "pennies for the class," and which pile was the "leftover pennies."

Melinda

I wondered about this way of solving the problems. It hadn't occurred
to me that children wouldn't count all the objects. It also hadn't occurred
to me that the problems *could* be done this way. I then wondered if it is
actually a more *natural* way for children; it certainly models what
happens in the problem. And kids might use this method because it lets
them think of two parts, without also having to hold the whole in the
picture. Indeed, why hadn't *I* thought of this obvious way to look at these
problems? I was really stuck on "whole minus part equals other part" as
the most natural method, and I assumed you had to know the whole to
figure out the answer.

Nate also solved the problems by dumping the contents of a bag,
separating out 26, and counting the remainder. He wanted to write a
number sentence to show his thinking, and he wanted it to be
subtraction. He separated 26 corks out of a collection and counted the
remaining 14. He kept saying, "So 26 – 14 is . . ." and then stopping, I
think because it did not make sense to him in the context of the problem.
When I asked him how many corks were in the bag, he figured it out by
adding 26 and 14 mentally. But he didn't want to write 26 + 14 = 40
because he wanted to subtract.

I wondered why he wanted to subtract. Was it a strong feeling he had
that this was a subtraction situation? Was it because there is "taking away"
in the problem? Had he heard other kids call it a subtraction problem?
Because our work time was ending, I didn't have time to keep going with
him, but I wondered if he realized that there is a relationship between
40 – 26 and 26 + 14. Was it clearer to him with the candy problem of
9 – 5 and 5 + 4? Was he aware of the pile of 14 being the "answer" to the
question asked? Did he see a relationship between the whole collection of
40 corks and the parts that were 26 corks and 14 corks?

I guess I'm a slow learner, because our most recent encounter with
"Enough for the Class" surprised me, too. This time there were 16 pink
cubes and 17 blue cubes in the bag. My preconception was that children
would add 16 and 17 and then somehow figure out what was left after
taking 26 out of that total.

Many children actually did solve the problem the way I expected. And
many didn't. Several children explained their strategy as some version of
the following, which was Nick's approach:

> Take 10 from the 16 and 10 from the 17. That's 20. Take the 6
> from the 16, and now you have 26, enough for the class. The 7
> from the 17 is left.

They showed a lovely ability and willingness to take numbers apart and put numbers together. They were clearly thoughtful about the problem and had made sense of what was being asked. But they still didn't figure out how many cubes there were in all!

I am not sure what surprises me more—that so many children don't think explicitly about the whole or the total when solving these problems, or that it never occurred to me that they didn't have to.

160

C A S E 10

Valentine stickers

Jody

When the children arrive each morning, right away they start work on the problem of the day, which I have written on a chart or on the chalkboard. One day last week, I had this word problem displayed:

165

? Sabrina and Yvonne have 14 stickers when they put their stickers together. Yvonne has 6 stickers. How many stickers does Sabrina have?

Solving the problem of the day has become a routine in my class; after settling in, the children just go and get any materials they need (cubes, links, counters) to solve the problem. They know that they have to keep a record of their strategies for solving the problem, using models, pictures, words, or number sentences, so that they would be able to explain their thinking process to someone else.

170

This is how Latasha, a first grader, solved the problem. First she drew 14 hearts on her paper (see next page). Then she wrote numbers 1 to 6 inside the first 6 hearts. Then she started again, writing from 1 to 8 on the remaining hearts. She marked off the first 6 hearts. Below her picture of hearts, she wrote 6 + 8 = 14.

175

180

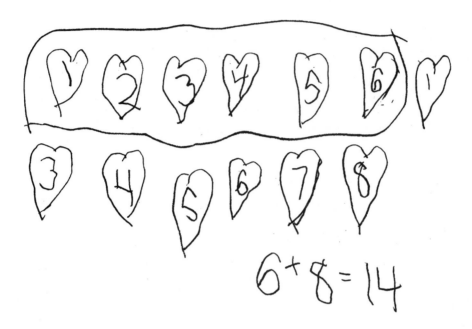

$$6 + 8 = 14$$

Most adults would think of this as a subtraction problem, but Latasha represented it with an addition sentence. When I saw what she was doing, I wanted to make sure that she was clear about her process and that she understood the problem. I asked Latasha what the 14 was. She said that this was the number of stickers Sabrina and Yvonne had together. When I asked her how many stickers Sabrina had, she quickly pointed to the hearts labeled 1 to 8 that she had not put a circle around and said, "Sabrina has 8 stickers." Her responses assured me that she understood what the problem was and that her strategy was clear to her.

Jessie, a second grader, did not draw a picture for this problem. Instead she wrote the following on her paper:

If Yvonne has 6 stickers and they have 14 altogether, I figured it out by minusing 6 from 14.

$14 - 6 = 8$

I also figured it out like this:

$6 + \underline{\quad} = 14$

I know that $6 + 6 = 12$, add 2 more $= 14$, so

$6 + 8 = 14$

Having known Jessie for over a year now, since she was in my first-grade class last year, I know that she feels comfortable explaining her thinking process using numbers. Sometimes she uses pictures or other representations, but for this particular problem she didn't, and I felt she understood the problem. Jessie is used to explaining different ways of solving a problem. The numbers involved in the problem were low enough that she could visualize them without having to use objects or pictures. She knows her number combinations and she was able to solve the problem with both addition and subtraction. She also used what she knows about doubles to get her answer.

Cecile, another second grader, did not use pictures or objects either. She explained her way like this:

I know that 7 + 7 = 14, so I took 1 from one of the 7s and put it on the other 7 so now it is 6 + 8 and it's 14.

I asked Cecile what she was thinking when she started with 7 + 7 = 14. She said, "7 + 7 is easier for me to think about and that makes 14, so if I move 1 from one of the 7s to the other, I have 6 + 8 and that is 14."

Cecile feels comfortable with renaming addends that add up to the same number. One of our daily routines is thinking of many different ways to rename a number using doubles, addition, and subtraction. Cecile often thinks of numbers that are easier and more convenient for her to deal with, to help her solve problems.

Maya is a first grader. For the sticker problem, she took 14 cubes and made a tower. Then she took 6 cubes and made another tower. She lined up the two towers next to each other, like this:

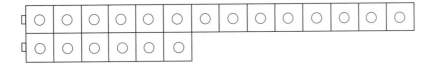

When she counted how many cubes there were beyond her 6-cube tower, she found that there were 8.

When I saw what Maya had done, I was struck by the fact that her model consisted of more than 14 cubes. I asked her what the 8 cubes represented, and she said it was Sabrina's stickers. She said that the 6-cube tower below the 14-cube tower was only a way for her to remember how many stickers Yvonne had. She was using the extra 6 cubes as a marker so that she could easily see how many stickers Sabrina had. I then asked her what the 14 cubes represented, and she said that these were the stickers that Yvonne and Sabrina had together. Maya could explain her process clearly by using objects, but when I asked her if she could tell me a math sentence that showed what she had just done, she was not able to do it.

Joachim, a second grader, had drawn this on his paper:

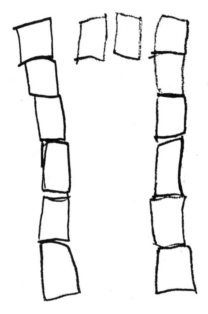

Joachim's model confused me at first, so I asked him to explain his process. This is what he said:

> I took two 6s and added them. That is 12. But this is not the correct number so I added 2 to the 12 and it is 14. So now it is 6 + 6 + 2 = 14. And 6 + 8 = 14.

Joachim's way is similar to Cecile's. They both relied on their knowledge of doubles to get to the right number.

I asked Damien, who had chosen to use a number strip, how he solved the problem. He put his finger on 6 and said, "I started counting up from 6 until I got to 14, and I counted 8." As I listened to him count, he said "1" as he pointed to 7, "2" as he pointed to 8, and kept moving up until he said "8" as he pointed to 14. Damien also made 14 circles on his paper and counted off 6 by putting a line across each of 6 circles. There were 8 circles left.

Antoinette used cubes to help her solve the problem. She explained her process like this:

> Since Yvonne has 6 stickers, I took 6 cubes. Then I said, how many more cubes should I take to get to 14, and then I counted up until I got to 14, and there were 8 more.

When I asked Antoinette to show me how she counted up from 6, she said, "6 . . . [*pause*], 7, 8, 9, 10, 11, 12, 13, 14." Her way of solving the problem is similar to Damien's first way. Although they had different materials, both used counting up to solve the problem.

Kim, a second grader, and Dylan, a first grader, were working together and role-playing the problem, pretending that one of them was Yvonne and the other was Sabrina. They counted 14 teddy bear counters together. Then Kim said, "I am Yvonne and you are Sabrina. I have 6 teddy bears. How many teddy bears do you have?" Dylan, acting as Sabrina, counted his teddy bears and he exclaimed, "I have 8. So Sabrina has 8 stickers!" They were having a good time pretending, and when I left them, I asked them to try to think of another way to solve the same problem.

All the children had appropriate solution methods. They used methods that were familiar to them; some used number combinations that were easy for them to think about. They understood the problem and

245

250

255

260

265

270

were able to explain their strategies and represent the problem in different ways. My goal for all my students is that they feel comfortable in communicating their thinking process while also expanding their repertoire of strategies for problem solving. I encourage them to try solving a problem in more than one way and to share their strategies with someone else. I also would like my students to explore the properties of addition and subtraction. Jessie, who used the operations, knew that the problem could be solved by either addition or subtraction.

275

C A S E 11

Rocks, trips, and writing groups

Dolores

GRADE 3, OCTOBER

Each new class and school year involves lots of getting to know each other and setting systems into place. The expectations for math in my classroom include being respectful of everyone's ideas (even errors), communicating about thinking, trying alternative strategies, being flexible with ideas and numbers, and enjoying the exploration of numbers during problem solving.

280

285

Every year I encounter the widely held belief that the faster you can get an answer, the smarter you are. And almost every year I encounter girls who have already come to believe that they can't do math or they don't get it. Much of my energy goes into ridding the class of those notions. Instead, students begin to feel that success is related to making mathematics make sense.

290

This year we have worked on several problems that caused many children to ask, "Do I add or take away?" The structure of my questions is not the typical form of providing two addends and asking for the sum, or giving a quantity and finding out what is left after some amount is taken away. Following are three of the word problems we have worked with so far.

295

Dolores

GRADE 3, OCTOBER

? I keep many rocks on my coffee table at home. Recently friends came by and brought me more. I am sure 27 of them are new. I now have 54 rocks. How can I find out how many rocks I had before my friends came?

300

? I took a trip to visit my dear friend who lives exactly 30 miles from my house. I used a trip counter in my car to know I stopped after precisely 15 miles to buy my friend a pumpkin. When I got back in my car I was wondering, like lots of kids always ask, are we there yet? and how much further? Can you tell how long the rest of the trip would be?

305

? Let's say there is a special writing group that our class could join if we had 37 kids. How many more kids would we need to find? [*Our class has 24 kids, a number all my students know from daily counting routines.*]

310

My students have come up with many ways to solve these problems. Initially, they all "needed" me to tell them whether to write an addition problem or a subtraction one, but they got no answer from me on that question. I did encourage them to find several different ways to go about it. I said, "I'll be interested to see how you solve it." They could decide on making pictures, setting up tally marks, arranging cubes, counting on their fingers, or writing calculations.

315

For the rock problem, quite a few children started individual work in their math journals by making 54 tally marks to stand for the rocks. Some crossed off the first 27 marks and others crossed off the last 27. They came out with 27, or some number that was very close to 27. (Writing or counting too fast or too slow has been recognized by the class as a pitfall to avoid.) Some others had written out a string of numbers from 1 through 54, crossed off 1 through 27, and renumbered 28 as 1, 29 as 2, and so forth.

320

325

Joshua was "all done" very quickly (see his work in Figure 6). I was curious about his work because we had read, reread, and paraphrased the question as a whole class before any work began. I was more than a little surprised to hear Joshua report that a previous teacher had said, "Just check for two numbers. If the first number is bigger, take away. If the first number is littler, add." OK. That was my first reminder this year that I'll always be asking kids to use logic and reasoning, which may very well be competing with "helpful hints" or "shortcuts" taught by others.

330

Dolores

GRADE 3, OCTOBER

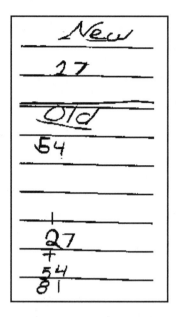

Figure 6. Joshua's work on the rock problem.

A few students, like Dimitri, drew rocks or dots to stand for rocks (see Figure 7). These students had 54 as the total in mind and put a space between 27 and the rest of the rocks needed to reach 54. They finished by counting up just the unknown amount beyond 27. There were some counting errors, which were quickly detected during group-sharing time. I was interested by the reaction of several children that 27 *couldn't* be the answer, because 27 was the number of new rocks and it couldn't be "right" for the number of old rocks, too. I wondered why. They weren't able to say; third graders need practice in articulating the reasons behind what they sense is right or not. We work on this constantly.

Several children tried to move from marks on their pages to the more abstract recording of what happened using only numbers, but they ran into difficulties; an example is Molly's work in Figure 8. The numbers on Molly's page do not reflect what her 54 Xs and tally marks show. She also lost the meaning of the 4 and 7 in 54 and 27, and simply took the smaller digit from the larger. This showed me an area where more understanding was needed. The context seemed to have been lost.

Making Meaning for Operations

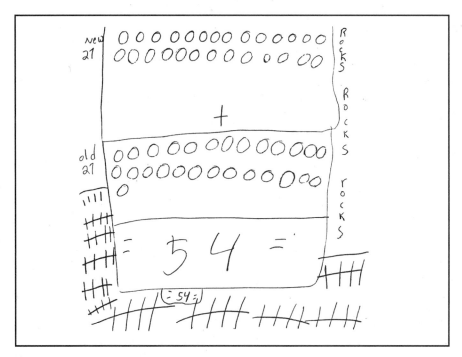

Figure 7. Dimitri's work on the rock problem.

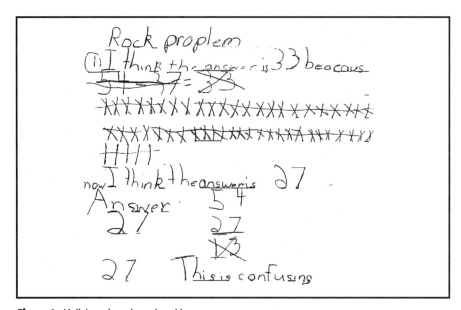

Figure 8. Molly's work on the rock problem.

Dolores

Another issue that appeared in students' work on all three problems involved knowing where to start counting on. Did counting on start at the 27th or the 28th rock? Did it start at the 15th or 16th mile? Did it start on the 24th child or the 25th?

For the problem involving the second stage of a 30-mile trip, Shareena first drew all the miles for the entire trip. Then she separated off the miles driven in the first stage of the trip by drawing a line after mile 15 (see Figure 9), and started counting the remainder at mile 16.

Some of my students were not able to take the mental leap to an abstracted concept of the first part to count onto. They needed the physical objects, marks, or numbers. By contrast, Allison (Figure 10) can count on and doesn't need to have the representation of 1 to 15. There is a certain level of confidence demonstrated by students when they know the 15 miles have been driven without showing them.

Allison and her partner Christopher changed the problem by stopping for coffee instead of a pumpkin, a change that doesn't affect the outcome at all. But when Christopher (Figure 11) tried to use the same reasoning as Allison, he ran into trouble. When he drew his representation of the rest of the trip after stopping for coffee, he counted the 15th mile as another mile traveled, rather than as the *starting point* to go to mile 16.

355

360

365

370

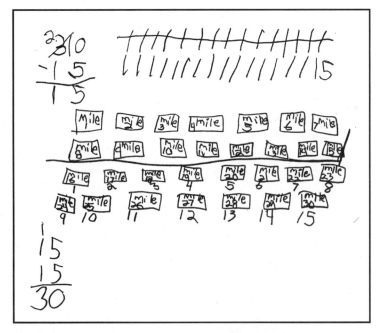

Figure 9. Shareena's work on the problem about the 30-mile trip made in two phases.

Making Meaning for Operations

Dolores

GRADE 3, OCTOBER

This gets rather complex as students try to decide if they are counting the mile markers themselves or the intervals between. Christopher did go on to see if 15 miles and another 16 miles would get us to the friend's house. Trouble was spotted and help was offered by peers.

375

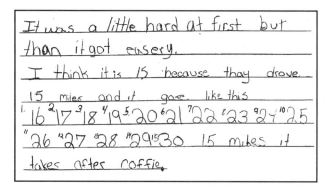

It was a little hard at first but than it got easery.
I think it is 15 because thay drove 15 miles and it gose like this
16 17 18 19 20 21 22 23 24 25 26 27 28 29 30 15 miles it takes after coffie.

Figure 10. Allison's work on the 30-mile-trip problem.

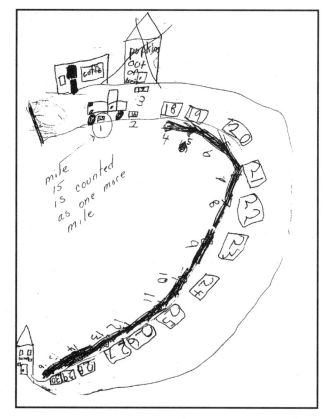

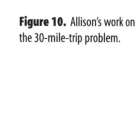

mile 15 counted is one more mile

Figure 11. Christopher's work on the 30-mile-trip problem.

Dolores

As I got to know some of my very quiet students, I learned that a few of them pretty much believed math meant "do anything with numbers ... I don't know why!" I frequently found children choosing any old calculation. What happened when they tried to answer some of these problems is typical of the troubles that a few third graders find themselves in each year. The calculation they wrote had no real meaning. Kalyn (Figure 12) was not visualizing a trip of 30 miles in length that had been partially completed; maybe she was partially remembering the rule Joshua had recited, about "find two numbers . . . ." But was the rule to add or take away? Kalyn's calculations don't fit the situation. I also have to wonder what subtraction really means to Kalyn if she can begin with 15, subtract 30, and still have 25. There seems to have been little, if any, expectation that this should make sense.

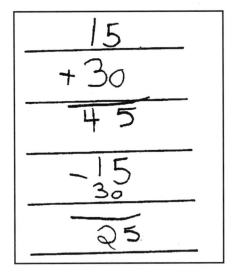

Figure 12. Kalyn's work on the 30-mile-trip problem.

By the time we got to the problem about needing 37 writers when we currently have 24, the class had spent many hours sharing solution strategies on other problems. They had shared work with partners and with the whole class. We had practiced how to ask questions if we disagreed with the work or the reasoning being shared by others. Luisa, who had previously written 27 – 54 = as the starting point for the rock problem, now solved the 37 writers problem by drawing 37 kids and

Making Meaning for Operations

circling our class of 24 (see Figure 13). Then she counted up the number of kids still needed to make 37. That was progress for this child.

Travis had needed to draw out 54 rocks for the first problem, and later needed to write out all 30 miles for the second one. Now, to solve the third problem, Travis listed just the numbers from 24 to 37, and he knew to count the 25th student as the first extra kid (see Figure 14).

400

Figure 13. Luisa's work on the writing-group problem.

Figure 14. Travis's work on the writing-group problem.

Dolores

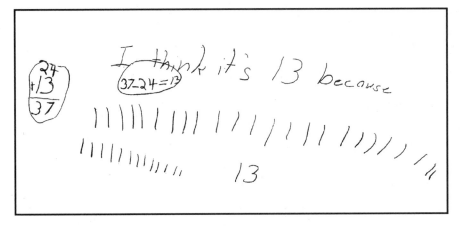

Figure 15. Doniel's work on the writing-group problem.

Several students moved back and forth between concrete representations and more abstract calculations. In Doniel's work on the third problem (Figure 15), he began to see the relationship between his tally marks and the two calculations of 24 + 13 = 37 and 37 − 24 = 13.

There is much work to do and many experiences to provide for this class. The first giant step has been for them to really believe that mathematics should make sense. Given that, everything else should be easier.

405

C H A P T E R

3

What is multiplication?
What is division?

As we move from the consideration of addition and subtraction to multiplication and division, the questions that were posed in chapters 1 and 2 still apply, and we extend them:

■ How can a single situation be represented by different number sentences?

■ When we see the different number sentences that can model a single situation, what do we learn about relationships among operations?

- What does it mean to have constructed concepts of the various operations?

Furthermore, multiplication and division come with their own questions:

- What kinds of situations are modeled by multiplication and division?

- What issues must students work through in order to make sense of these operations?

- What ideas about addition and subtraction do students bring to their work with multiplication and division?

Ponder and take notes on these questions as you read the following cases from grades 2 through 5.

C A S E **12**

What is multiplication?

Linda

GRADE 4, DECEMBER

As we turned away from our intense study of subtraction, I was curious to find out what my fourth graders knew about multiplication. What did they think it was? How was it different from the operations we had just been studying? These were questions I had been thinking about for myself as well as for my students, and I hadn't come to any solid conclu-   5
sions yet.

From previous conversations, I had learned that multiplication, to most of these students, means a chart of facts—The Tables. Some children are happy with this definition because, since they know their facts, they "know" multiplication. Others are less comfortable with this definition   10
because they've seen the chart but have not memorized it. I myself am unsure about the place of the multiplication facts in an understanding of multiplication. I know that even if students have mastery of the facts, that doesn't mean they necessarily understand what happens to different

amounts when they are multiplied. But I'm also aware that knowing the facts makes life easier for children; besides, other teachers will expect students to know them. I decided to begin our study of multiplication by looking at the facts and trying to give them some meaning.

I flashed a large multiplication fact chart (through the 10s) on the overhead and suggested that we could eliminate the need to learn every individual fact by looking for patterns and relationships. After some discussion, the class came to the following conclusions:

Any number times 0 is 0.

Any number times 2 is that number doubled.

Everyone knows the 5s table from playing games.

We know the 10s by taking a number and putting a 0 in the ones place.

Any fact given backwards has the same answer as given forwards. ($5 \times 2 = 10$, $2 \times 5 = 10$)

Any number times 1 is that same number.

Viviana caused some debate by offering a revision of the last point, suggesting that "any number times 1 is always the bigger number." I asked her to prove that and she came to the board and wrote:

$1 \times 8 = 8$ $1 \times 7 = 7$ $1 \times 9 = 9$

It seemed true to her and most of the class was satisfied, but a couple of students looked puzzled. Kazuo wondered about 1×1 because, "What number is the bigger one?" In response, we heard "Oh" from a few students, but not much further discussion.

Then Tyrel said, "Wait—0×1 makes what Viviana said not true, because 1 is the bigger number but the answer is 0." At this point, the class decided to go with the earlier version of the last point.

As a result of these discussions, we came up with the following pared-down list of multiplication facts to memorize:

3×3	4×4	6×6	7×7	8×8	9×9
3×4	4×6	6×7	7×8	8×9	
3×6	4×7	6×8	7×9		
3×7	4×8	6×9			
3×8	4×9				
3×9					

The students were now satisfied that once they knew the answers to those facts, they would "know" multiplication. Since the period was over, I left them with that understanding, but asked them to think about whether or not there was more to multiplication than just a list of facts.

The next day I began math by asking, "If multiplication is more than a chart of facts, what is it?"

Claudia answered, "A tool for math."

Tyrel suggested, "A faster way to add."

"How is multiplication a faster way to add?" I asked the class. In the back of my mind, I'm wondering, why isn't multiplication an *action* for the students, the way adding is? Why is it a *thing*—a tool or a shortcut?

Then Kadeem spoke up. "I want to talk about what Tyrel said, about a faster way to add. What if you wanted to find out 100 plus 5 more, fast? How would you multiply?"

I thought that was a great question, but the class didn't take it on. Instead, Kandi said that she wanted to show 50×5. She went to the board and wrote:

$$\begin{array}{r} 50 \\ \underline{\times 5} \\ 100 \end{array}$$

Then Kandi explained, "5 plus 5 is 10 and 0 times 5 equals 0. Add 0 on the end of 10 and you get 100."

Rashana said, "I need to show what I think. 5 times 50 is not 100." She went to the board and wrote:

$$\begin{array}{r} 50 \\ \underline{\times 5} \\ 250 \end{array}$$

Explaining her work, Rashana said, "5 times 0 is 0. 5 times 5 is 25."

Eric disagreed, saying, "I don't understand what Rashana means, but I do understand what Kandi said. The answer is 100."

This discussion continued for the rest of the period, and in the end the class seemed to conclude that the answer to 50×5 is 250. However, I'm not satisfied with the arguments that were offered for one position or another. I think the children who were most confident about the procedures they memorized last year convinced the rest of the group. I am still left wondering, What *is* multiplication? What should my students understand about that operation? And how will they learn it?

How do kids think about division?

Georgia

In the past I have begun the year by having kids do projects, such as making maps or building pendulums, that integrate math topics with other areas of the curriculum. I did this because I wanted to see what ideas kids were thinking about before I began pursuing my own agenda. Kids were certainly invested and interested in the projects, but the specific math topics that I could expect to be covered were unpredictable. Although I love to teach math this way, and there is great potential in this approach, I decided instead to begin this year by focusing on the four operations. I shifted away from a project-based math curriculum so I could study the mathematics the children were doing. I chose to give my own creative ideas a rest to investigate the children's ideas more closely.

As I discussed my plan with a colleague, she seemed reassured by this steady, reliable way of thinking about math. Last year she clearly didn't trust that kids would get enough exposure to the four basic operations while pursuing big, in-depth projects. So she was feeling comforted—until I said I was particularly interested in learning how my eight-, nine-, and ten-year-old students thought about division. This horrified her, because she believes that children need to be taught the operations in a certain order. In her mind, first comes addition, then multiplication, then subtraction, then division.

My initial idea was just to expose kids to division problems early in their experience with numbers so that the process would be familiar when they came to the numbers that themselves implied division— decimals and fractions. But, through my classroom research, I'm learning much more about how kids think about division, what they call division, and how they define division. Much of this learning comes from my observations of their written work.

Each week I have given the students story problems that I considered to be division problems, problems I myself would solve by using division. Here are some examples of the problems and some kids' responses to them.

? Jesse has 24 shirts. If he puts eight of them in each drawer, how many drawers does he use?

Vanessa wrote: $24 - 8 = 16$, $16 - 8 = 8$, $8 - 8 = 0$, and then wrote 3 for the answer.

? If Jeremy needs to buy 36 cans of seltzer water for his family and they come in packs of six, how many packs should he buy?

This time Vanessa wrote: $6 + 6 = 12$, $12 + 12 = 24$, $24 + 6 = 30$, $30 + 6 = 36$. I still need to ask her how many packs that gives her. But what made her add this time and subtract last time?

Other students use these same methods. Is it significant that sometimes they add and sometimes they subtract? What are their choices based on? I thought the problems about Jesse's shirts and the six-packs of seltzer water were the same kind of problem, and yet students treated them differently. On reflection, I wonder if the total number (24 or 36 in this case) affects how kids approach the problem. If the total number is a familiar one, do they subtract (until they get zero), and if the number is less familiar, do they add, building up to the number, as Vanessa did for the second problem?

? Joni wants to build some bookshelves for her friends and family. If she bought 36 boards and she needs 4 boards for each bookshelf, how many bookshelves is she going to make?

Cory had clearly tried approaching this problem more than one way. His paper was filled with tally marks, which seemed to be one way he was thinking about it, while above the problem he had written $2 \div 36 = 28 \div 2 = 14$. I decided to ask him about his thinking. I assumed he meant $36 \div 2 = 28$, but I wasn't sure how he got the 28. I wanted to find out how he was really thinking about the problem instead of making assumptions.

Cory told me, "I thought it was times." Then he reread the problem aloud. "See, that's why I changed it to divided by. If it was 4 divided by, I would probably use 2 first so it would be easier. First I would do 2 divided by 36, and that equals 28, and 2 divided by 28 equals 14, so that's how I came up with 14. Because I knew divided by is half of whatever the number is, like 2 divided by 100 is 50."

I asked Cory, "Does that mean that 28 is half of 36?"

"Yes," he said, "because I know half of 30 is . . . wait a second . . . no, that isn't right. It would be 15 plus another 3, that's probably 18 and divided by that, which is 9."

Cory knew that 36 is made up of 30 and 6, and half of 30 is 15, and half of 6 is 3. Then he knew that 15 plus 3 is 18. He understands division in terms of halving, as he clearly states: "Divided by is half of whatever the number is." Halving is also implicit in his comment, "That's probably 18 and divided by that, which is 9"; he doesn't even have to say he halved it. And he knows that dividing by 4 is like halving twice. What about division that isn't based on half? Would that be division to him? What will happen when he has to divide by 3?

? You go into a pet store that sells mice. There are 48 mouse legs. How many mice are there?

Matthew organized his work beautifully. He wrote a key (m = mice, l = legs) and put his numbers in columns.

$$1\,m \quad 4\,l$$
$$2\,m \quad 8\,l$$
$$3\,m \quad 12\,l$$
$$4\,m \quad 16\,l$$
$$5\,m \quad 20\,l$$
$$6\,m \quad 24\,l$$
$$7\,m \quad 28\,l$$
$$8\,m \quad 32\,l$$
$$9\,m \quad 36\,l$$
$$10\,m \quad 40\,l$$
$$11\,m \quad 44\,l$$
$$12\,m \quad 48\,l$$

Then in a neat box he wrote, "12 m × 4 l = 48 l." Above the box he wrote the number 12. What does this say about Matthew's understanding of division? He knows that 12 is the answer, but he feels satisfied with a multiplication number sentence in which the answer is *part* of the problem rather than the *answer* to the problem. He knows how to find the answer, but instead of the number sentence I had expected, 48 ÷ 4 = 12, he wrote a multiplication number sentence.

During a conversation with classmates about a similar problem, Matthew said, "This is another division problem. It's 63 divided by 9. What number times 9 is 63? Seven." When I asked him to explain what there was about the problem that made it a division problem, he said, "I don't know, but it is. But my thinking is multiplication." | 185

What does this say about kids' understanding of division if they use all the operations *except* division? As I look at how kids think about division, and how I had initially hoped that the work would help kids with fractions, I wonder in what way the two topics are connected. Do kids bump up against the same ideas in both division and fraction work? | 190
What does this say about how kids think about wholes and parts?

C A S E **14**

More insects and spiders

Mandy

I wanted my second graders to explore larger numbers and multiples of things. I thought they would solve these problems by counting, and I hoped that this would be an exposure to or a beginning for thinking about multiplication. | 195

I assigned partners and gave each pair a worksheet I had devised, "A Farmer's Problem." In this first problem, the farmer is in his pasture assessing how many legs and how many tails there are on 6 chickens and 5 cows.

Michael and Diego worked together. (Refer to Figure 16 for their | 200
work.) They talked it over and drew 6 simple chickens, showing just a body and 2 legs, and wrote 12. They drew 5 cows, depicting a simple body with a head and 4 legs. They wrote the labels *chickens* and *cows* and their answer, *32 legs*. Although they did not write 20 to reflect 20 legs on the cows, their drawings show the right number, and the 32 is circled and | 205
correctly labeled *legs.*

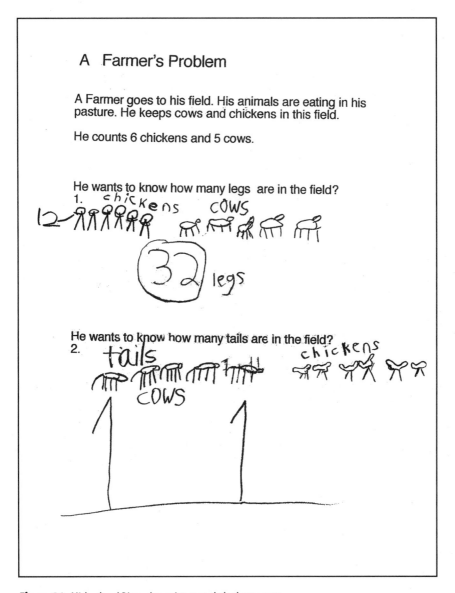

Figure 16. Michael and Diego draw pictures to help them count.

Michael and Diego then went on to a second worksheet, "A Farmer's Problem II," with 7 pigs and 15 geese (see Figure 17). For the first question about tails, they drew simple figures and counted 22 tails. They wrote *tails* above the drawings and the answer 22 below (but did not label the answer with *tails*).

210

Chapter 3

59

A Farmer's Problem II

The very next day the Farmer goes to his pig pen in the barn cellar. The pigs (like Wilbur) and the geese live in the barn cellar.

He counts 7 pigs and 15 geese.

He wants to know how many tails are in the barn cellar?

1.

He wants to know how many legs are in the barn cellar?

2.

$$28 + 30 = 58 \text{ legs}$$

Figure 17. When time runs out, Michael and Diego switch from pictures to an equation to find the answer.

For the leg question, they simply wrote 28 + 30 = 58 legs. These boys drew careful pictures for the first three questions, but as their time ran out, they made an equation. Their equation is correct and they labeled their answer *58 legs,* showing that they knew that they were counting legs, not geese or pigs.

Another day, I gave children a worksheet asking about the number of legs in a group of ants and spiders. They worked on this individually rather than with partners.

Jake's work (Figure 18) shows clearly that he understands how to add in groups. He first drew 7 ants and 1 spider; then he circled 4 ants, which he labeled 24 [legs]; 3 ants, which he labeled 18; and 1 spider. He wrote 6 + 6 + 6 + 6 + 6 + 6 + 6 + 8 and, below that, 50.

A Spider Problem

In Charlotte's Web Charlotte weaves webs to catch food
and to save Wilbur's life.

1. How many legs does Charlotte have?___8___

 An ant is an insect   (not an arachnid), so an ant
has 6 legs.

You need this information to be able to answer the
questions that follow.

2. One day Charlotte was waiting near her web when 7
ants walked by the barn cellar.

Counting Charlotte and the 8 ants: How many legs were
there? 24

6 + 6+ 6 + 6+ 6 + 6 + 6 + 8

50

Figure 18. Jake moves towards multiplication by adding ant legs in groups of 6.

When I asked him how he got the 50, he said that he added the
24 + 18 + 8.

I said, "Tell me in words how you did it."

Jake explained, "This is 10 [*pointing at the 18*] and I put it with the 20 of
24, which makes 30. Then I took the 8 from the 18 and added it to the 4
[*from the 24*]; that made 12. So I added 10 of the 12 to the 30 to make 40. I
put the 2 [*from the 12*] and added it to the 8 of the spider. That's 10, so 40
and 10 is 50." He smiled, pleased that his thinking was correct.

225

230

Candy canes for the school

Janine
GRADE 4, DECEMBER

The variety I see in the ways my students solve problems sometimes amazes me. Some of the students will immediately run for the blocks or the calculator without even giving a thought to what is needed. Some set out drawing pictures. Some work solely with the numbers (some smartly, and some just trying to put the numbers together). Some have no idea how to even begin the problem unless I come over and give them a jump start.

How do I get them to become problem solvers? How do I get them to think about what's being asked? How do I get them to be self-motivated, especially when the concepts are hard? How do I get them to really *see* a problem and all its components?

Well, they're getting better! More and more of the students are finding their way into the problems on their own. They are beginning to seek out partners that they can work with, rather than just their friends. They are becoming more and more motivated at least to try. They are beginning to ask themselves their own questions and are beginning to listen to one another. We still have a long way to go, but progress is being made.

I sat with three girls today as they tried to tackle the following problem:

> **?** There are 609 students at the school. How much would it cost to buy each one a candy cane? Candy canes are sold in packages of 6 for $ .29.

I have been trying to make the rounds and sit with a different group each day. It's interesting to see who has the concepts, who sits back, who leads the discussion, who is totally lost, which ones listen to each other, and which ones hear only their own voice.

The threesome that I sat with today is a new grouping. They have never worked together before, but they seemed to click on this problem.

235

240

245

250

255

Janine

They started out each working on her own for a few minutes, and then began talking. Almost immediately the three decided that the problem had something to do with the 6 times tables—and that they had to go pretty far up the table to get to where they wanted to be. They started 6, 12, 18, 24, 30, and soon realized that there had to be a faster way.

Letitia, who grasps concepts pretty quickly, suggested that they should do 90×6 because, she figured out, that would be 540. Wow! Good for her, I thought. We have been working on multiplying numbers by multiples of 10, so I guess this clicked for her: $6 \times 9 = 54$, so 6×90 would equal 540. I was hoping she would take it one step further and see that 6×100 would be 600, but she stopped there and neither of the other two saw this either. Maybe this is because, when studying the 6 tables in third grade, they only went up to 6×9.

From 540 they decided that they had to add up by 6s to get to 609. This is where keeping track of their numbers became *very* difficult. Letitia, after some thought, said that $540 + 10$ more would equal 600. One of the others said that $540 + 10$ is equal to 550 and not 600. Letitia struggled to explain. She had the idea that 10 groups of 6 would get her to 600, but she kept confusing *10* and *10 groups of 6*. I could see her struggling to keep track of her thoughts; I could see her "getting it" and then having it fly out of her mind. She knew that 10 was important, but couldn't hold onto the idea that it wasn't 10 but *10 groups of 6* she was thinking about.

To help her out a little, I asked how many more she needed to get to 600 from 540. She answered 60. "Oh yeah—60 is 10 groups of 6!" She would grasp this idea for a while and then lose it again. She was really trying hard to hold onto the meaning of this 10!

So now they had 90 packages and 10 packages for a total of 600 candy canes. They knew they needed 9 more candy canes. One more package would bring them to 606, but they still needed 3 more. Could they buy 3 separately? No, they came in boxes of 6. If they bought another box, they would have 3 extra. What would they do with them? Natalia said, "Let's just eat them! We did the shopping. We deserve a prize!" All happily agreed that they would eat the 3 extras themselves.

Finally the group established that they had to buy $90 + 10 + 2$ packages of candy canes. Because they didn't know how to multiply $102 \times \$ .29$, they decided to do it with the calculator. Their answer came out 2958, which they reasoned would be $29.58.

I asked Letitia to write up what she and her group had done (see Figure 19). In the meantime, Natalia looked back at her original work on the problem and announced, "Oh, I made a mistake—big time!" What she had done (see Figure 20) was to skip count by sixes:

300

6   12   18   24   30   36   42   48   54   60   66   72   78   84   90

96   102   108   204   300   306   402   408   504   600   606   609

She counted 27 numbers and thought she would need 27 boxes of candy canes, but when she multiplied 27×6 she got only 162. Where was her

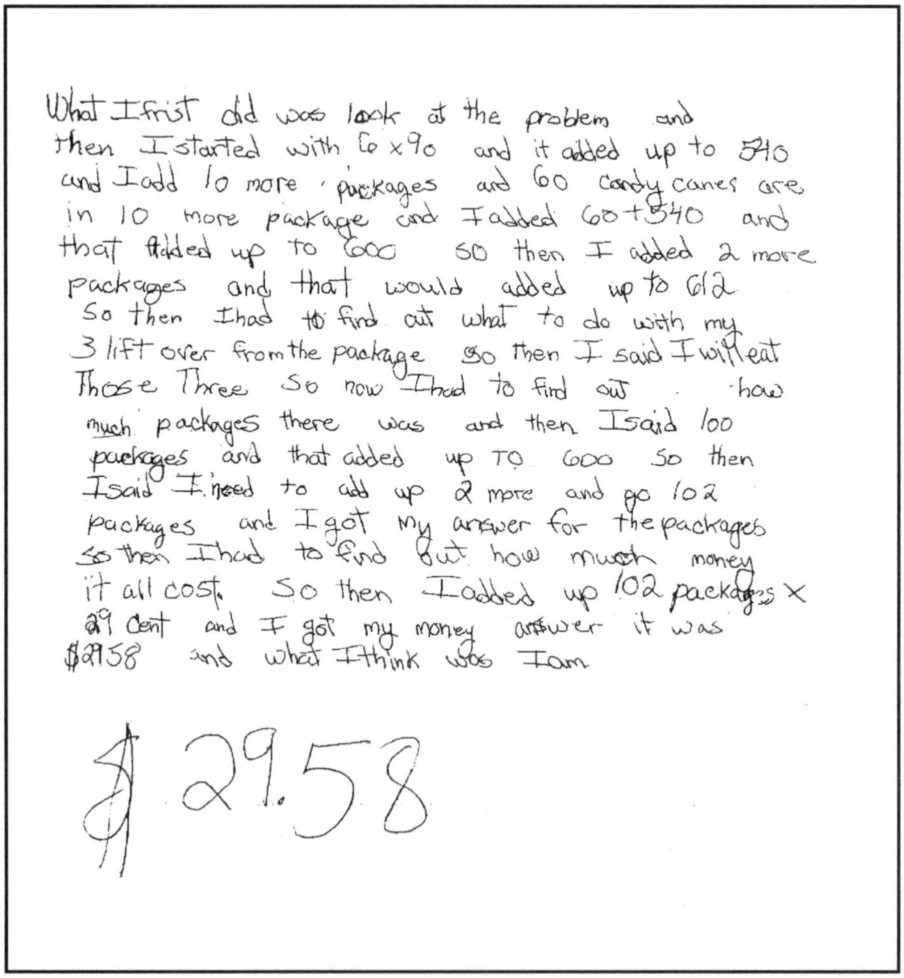

305

Figure 19. Letitia's write-up, showing how she and her group solved the candy cane problem.

Making Meaning for Operations

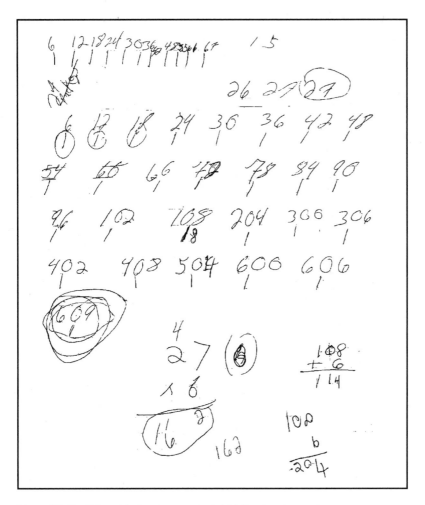

Figure 20. Natalia's work before the group started thinking together as a team.

mistake? Everything looked fine until she jumped from 108 to 204. How did she do this?

108	204	306	408
+ 6	+ 6	+ 6	+ 6
204	300	402	504

Looking back, Natalia discovered that she had added wrong, "big time" as she put it. If she had not gone back to see what she had done wrong, she may never have noticed the confusion she had when adding with 0 in the tens place.

310

My question remains—would these three motivated girls have gotten this far had I not been sitting with them to probe, push, ask questions, try to help clear up confusions? How can I get all my students to think hard without my being there *with* them? How do I get them to ask their own questions? How do I get them to stick with a problem even when it's difficult? Maybe it's just time and experience? Luckily, most of the students eagerly await the challenging problems I give them each week. Maybe that's the start in itself.

315

320

C A S E   16

Student drawings for 12 ÷ 4

Valerie

GRADE 5, OCTOBER

I asked my students to come up with a drawing for the problem $4 \overline{)12}$ and to explain their answers. After listening to their explanations and analyzing their drawings, I came to the conclusion that few, if any, actually understand what division is. They have been shown a procedure to follow and have tried to apply it, step by step.

325

All of the students were able to give the correct answer, but only one or two could tell me where the solutions came from and why. Some of the students simply plugged in objects in place of the numbers. So, for $4 \overline{)12}$, they would show something like this:

Others had no idea what to do and so just drew 12 objects.

Still other students could draw a good, representative picture (like the one below), and show the steps for long division, but could not verbalize what the picture showed.

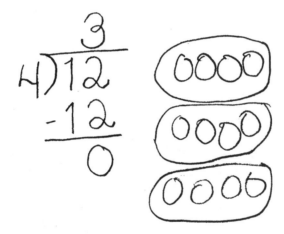

Only one student in the class could both draw a picture representing the problem *and* explain what he had done. He drew this:

Then he explained, "Say you would like some eggs, and you would like 4 in a group, and you have 3 boxes of eggs. That would come up to 12 eggs."

Valerie

GRADE 5, OCTOBER

It is clear to see these students have had very little, if any, experience using manipulatives, exploring mathematical ideas, or discussing mathematical thinking. The lack of these experiences has left them simply following steps with no understanding, kind of like little droids. If this were to continue, I feel it is only a matter of time until the majority of these students lose interest and just stop doing the math. It is my challenge to try to change that.

340

345

C A S E   17

Are these kids or seeds?

Melinda

GRADE 2, NOVEMBER

On Halloween I had my second graders work on this word problem:

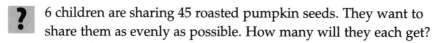 6 children are sharing 45 roasted pumpkin seeds. They want to share them as evenly as possible. How many will they each get?

I have to say first that I was really amazed and impressed with the industry and confidence with which the children approached the problem. Almost everyone got right to work and seemed to be engaged. Here are some things that seemed interesting to me.

350

Maria, Nikita, and Su-Yin worked together. They each got 45 Multilink™ cubes and snapped them together in a row. Su-Yin's initial strategy involved taking one cube off her collection of 45 so that she would have an even number left. When I asked her why she wanted an even number, she said so she could divide it in half. I asked her why she wanted to divide it in half, and what she planned to do next. She said she didn't know. I wondered whether she had some idea that she might be able to split her two even groups into three groups each somehow. On the other hand, maybe dividing something fairly made her think of halves and even numbers, without having any specific thought about needing six groups.

355

360

I never did find out, because Nikita and Maria had a different strategy, which Su-Yin adopted. Maria started making 6 piles of cubes, first breaking off a stick of 5 cubes for each. She then gave each pile 2 more, and had 3 cubes left.

I left these three girls for a while and worked with other children. When I returned to them, Maria was working by herself, drawing her 6 piles of 7 cubes, and Nikita and Su-Yin were arguing. Nikita was saying that each child got 7 seeds, and Su-Yin was saying each got 6, and that Nikita was counting a kid as a seed. Su-Yin indicated her 6 piles of cubes and asked me, "Are these kids or seeds?" I asked her what she meant, and she said that Nikita thought that they were all seeds, but that she had made each of her groups by putting a cube to be a kid in the center and then putting seeds around it. Therefore, her groups were 6 seeds and 1 kid each.

I was interested in Su-Yin's plan for representing and solving the problem, and I wondered what she had thought about in the process. I asked her to explain and show me exactly what she had done and thought from the beginning. She said she got 45 cubes, then put the 45 cubes in a big pile and made sure there were 45. I asked her why she had to have 45, and she said, "That's how many seeds there are." She explained then that she wanted to make groups by putting a kid in the middle and putting seeds around it, so she started to take cubes from the 45, and then said, "Oh! I need to get 6 more cubes!" I asked her why, and she said, "Because those *are* seeds!"

My question is, Is this about keeping track of units again? Su-Yin had to keep track of the numbers 45 and 6 from the start of this problem, and eventually there were some 7s and a 3. She had to think not just of the numbers and how they relate to each other, but also what they represent in this problem. I think that her plan to represent a child and then give the child a fair share of cubes representing seeds was a good one.

But was it too much for her to hold onto at once? First she didn't realize that she couldn't take any of the 45 cubes to make children, because those 45 represented the whole collection of seeds. Then, in her representation, she thought each group of 7 cubes showed a child and his or her seeds, still not realizing that "children" couldn't be taken from the "seeds," and that all the cubes had to be counted as seeds in the end. It was a lot to hold onto!

Melinda

I am also intrigued by the fact that Nikita and Su-Yin were so clear about what they were disagreeing about. Su-Yin's statement that Nikita was turning a kid into a seed showed some clarity about what was going on and where the confusion was, even though it was in fact *she* who had turned a seed into a kid. I also wonder why Nikita was so sure she was right about the problem, the solution, and her representation of them, but could not convince Su-Yin.

Meanwhile, Derrick and William were having an interesting time with the problem. William, who is fairly able but not very confident, said immediately, "I have an idea!" His idea, which he shared with Derrick, was to start with 45 and keep taking off 6s. They did *not* want to use manipulatives or draw pictures. They did use William's plan, and subtracted 6 repeatedly from 45 "in their heads." They ended up with a list of numbers, run together and hard to read:

45 39 33 27 21 15 9 3

William did say that he took out 6s because that was 1 seed for each child. I wasn't sure whether their list of numbers told him how many seeds each child ended up with, but my colleague Lydia was in the room, and she had a conversation with him about it. She later explained to me that he started to divide their list of numbers in a way to show that each time he subtracted 6, he was giving each child 1 seed. However, he made a mistake about where to divide the run-together numerals, and ended up with 6 groups. It didn't bother him that the numbers he created by dividing up his string did not make sense in the context of the problem.

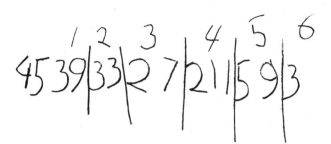

Making Meaning for Operations

Melinda

GRADE 2, NOVEMBER

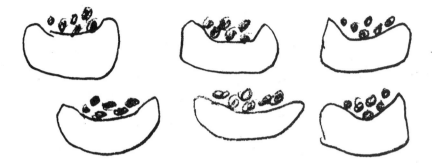

When I joined William and Derrick, they had their list of numbers and had drawn 6 little bowls with 6 little seeds in each. I asked them what the bowls were and how many seeds they had in their picture. William replied that the bowls were the seeds for each kid. Derrick figured out how many seeds they had drawn by adding 6s, and said there were 36. William agreed. Neither boy seemed bothered by the fact that they had accounted for only 36 seeds, when there were 45 in the problem.

I asked them, "How many seeds would be left then?" They figured out that there would be 9 by counting on from 36 up to 45. When I asked what they could "do" with the extra 9 seeds, they disagreed. William suggested that each child could have one more seed, but Derrick said, "No, there's only enough for one kid. You would need another kid." I asked why, and he said because there was only "one more 6." He decided that maybe one of the existing kids could get 6 more seeds, or 12 total, and that 3 could be thrown out. For some reason, he was unwilling to divide up a group of 6 seeds in order to give each child one more.

Apparently Derrick convinced William to give one person 12 and everyone else 6 (perhaps because I joked that maybe one of the kids was bossy or bigger or hungrier). When William explained his thinking to the class (I had him put out cubes to show his bowls of seeds), he had a group of 12 and 5 groups of 6. He went back and forth between labeling his groups of 6 as one seed for each kid and as a single kid's share of seeds. I think he was confused because he initially took out groups of 6 with a plan to give one seed in the group to each kid, and to do this as many times as possible, but then began to see those original piles of 6 as the seeds *for* each kid. I wondered why he didn't distribute 6 of the remaining 9 seeds in the end. Why did he stop distributing seeds when each of the 6 kids had 6?

Melinda

Again, I have questions about how children can keep the "whole" group of seeds in mind while they think of particular ways to divide it into parts. There are many issues for children to sort out: As they start dividing up the whole, what do their groups mean? Are they collections for each child? One seed for each child? Are the children themselves represented in their diagram or model of the problem? Although there were many confusions while these second graders worked on the problem, I have to say that they were remarkably able to make sense of a very complex question.

455

460

C H A P T E R

4

When dividing gives an answer less than one

| CASE 18 | Can you divide 39 into 5? | MaryAnn, Grade 4, April |
| CASE 19 | Can you divide 39 into 5? revisited | MaryAnn, Grade 5, November |

The action of sharing provides a context in which children can learn about the meaning of division. It also allows them to sort out some of the complexities of dividing whole numbers: What happens when the numbers don't divide evenly? Is it even possible to divide a larger number into a smaller? What sense could that possibly have?

In this chapter, we visit the same class twice as it explores what $5 \div 39$ might mean. In the spring of fourth grade, the students think about the question only in terms of whole numbers. What contexts are modeled by $5 \div 39$, and what would be the result of dividing 5 by 39? When they return to the question several months later as fifth graders, they are ready to consider their answer in terms of fractions. But their explorations now raise a new set of fascinating questions. As you read about these students' discussions, what ideas about division are highlighted for you? What new ideas must children entertain as they extend their work to the realm of fractions? And what ideas are *you* left to work through for yourself?

C A S E   18

Can you divide 39 into 5?

MaryAnn
GRADE 4, APRIL

This year I came to understand much more deeply what it means to engage my students in discussion of mathematical ideas. I have become convinced that attention to mathematical thinking will serve them much better than drill on computational procedures. However, as the metropolitan standardized test approaches, I am concerned. It matters to the lives of these inner-city children that they score well. The test does not assess how thoughtful they are about the meaning of the mathematics they do. Rather, it tests their speed and accuracy on arithmetic facts and procedures—what we've called "mastery" in the past.

For this reason, I decided to dedicate several weeks to the kind of problems they would face on the test. I distributed the textbook I have used in the past and assigned pages of drill. The day we were working on the "Division with Remainders" page, however, I realized that once we had entered the realm of ideas, we would never be far away from it. The session went like this.

TEACHER: Leo, what is problem 9? [*It's such a simple problem, I am almost not listening to the response.*]

LEO: 5 divided by 39.

The problem on the page reads 39 ÷ 5. Hoping that Leo will correct himself, I ask him to repeat his statement, but he sticks with the same response. I ask the class if they agree with Leo, and they all say yes. Is this important? Should I restate the problem correctly? Are the children simply being inattentive or does this indicate a deeper lack of understanding?

TEACHER: What would the answer to the problem 5 divided by 39 look like? [*All hands go up. I call on Keesha.*] 25

KEESHA: 7 remainder 4.

TEACHER: If the problem is 5 divided by 39, is 7 remainder 4 the answer?

The students all say that it is. I wait for a while; we all wait for a 30
while. The fact that we haven't moved on forces the students to review their work. They're beginning to realize they can take a risk here and discuss foggy ideas.

T.C.: The number will be like—I say zero. You can't divide 5 with a 39 'cause it's a higher number. You can't divide a number 35
that's lower by one that's higher.

At this point, the rest of the group seems to be neither convinced nor unconvinced but rather restlessly disinterested. They seem uncomfortable with my sticking with the same problem when they are all so sure the answer is 7 r 4. I am uncomfortable, too, and I wonder what they are so 40
"sure" of.

I have Clarence repeat what T.C. said, and he states it correctly. The other students all agree that he has verbalized the statement accurately, but no one seems to have a feeling for what it means, whether it works or doesn't work, or how it might translate in a context. I sense that they are 45
thinking only about rules for numbers without making a connection to what the problem means.

TEACHER: Is it true that you can't divide a small number by a large number?

ALEJANDRO: Yes, that's true. 5 can't divide by 39. If you had 39 kids and 5 50
dollars, you can't do that in a fair way. You will give 1 dollar to 5 persons and the other people will be mad.

I'm glad that Alejandro has introduced a context for us to think about. I'm also glad to hear him use the word "fair" and hope that the others will be triggered to think of the "fair shares" we had been studying not so many weeks ago.

DEON: He's right, because the answer will be something about zero 'cause there is no answer for a problem like that.

Well, the kids didn't pick up on fair shares. Now I wonder about Deon's idea that if there is no answer, then the answer is zero. Does zero make sense to him in the problem $5 \div 39$? Is zero the answer to the number sentence, or does zero mean there are no answers? Is the distinction between the two clear to him or to the others?

JACKSON: You cannot do 5 divided by 39 because on a calculator it won't work out. It will come out to be a number in the minus. It will be . . . .

Jackson's voice drops and then he stops. It seems that everyone is confused and few have any sense of the difference between $39 \div 5$ and $5 \div 39$. How could they have sat for days, apparently comfortably, doing whole pages of these traditional exercises? What has happened to all our thinking and discussing and the conclusions that we drew when we worked on fractions? What is their sense about the numbers here? I ask whether it might help to think of another context. Deon is tentative but offers one.

DEON: Well, 5 people and 39 desks. . . . [*He's not sure how to go on.*]

CYNTHIA: What T.C. said is true. If there were 39 principals and I had 5 pieces of candy to give them, then only 5 principals could have a piece. The other 34 would be mad at me and I would lose my job.

As I'm trying to sort out why Cynthia is subtracting, I'm also wondering about whether I should introduce another context. What if there were 39 principals and 5 pizzas? Would that context help them to think in terms of fractions? What if I made the problem simpler: 1 pizza and 4 kids? I suggest both examples, but the children don't pursue them.

SHANNON: 5 divided by 39 really gets me confused. I can't see it in my mind.

Shannon goes to the board. I ask her to write 5 divided by 39, but she writes $39 \div 5$. She just doesn't want to confront what seems so foreign to her. She keeps writing $39 \div 5$ no matter how many times we rephrase the problem. She says that she doesn't want to stretch any more and asks to sit down. It's time to end the lesson. | 90

Throughout today's class, many children just couldn't see that $39 \div 5$ and $5 \div 39$ model two different situations. Those who could see the difference decided that 5 could not be divided by 39 because there was no fair way to do it. I wasn't sure what to do. Is this something to follow up | 95 tomorrow, or should I continue with my agenda of preparing for the metropolitan exam?

C A S E **19**

Can you divide 39 into 5? revisited

MaryAnn

GRADE 5, NOVEMBER

This year I am in the fortunate position to have moved up a grade, together with my class. That is, the children I had last year in fourth grade are with me again this year as fifth graders. I am very pleased. | 100 They are delightful children, a pleasure to be with two years in a row. At the beginning of the year, we had much less work to do to establish norms of being in class together; there was already a sense of community among us. The several children who were new needed a couple of weeks to catch on, but they had good models in their classmates. This is | 105 especially helpful since we have some difficult circumstances to work with. For example, my class of 28 children is very unbalanced by gender: 21 boys and 7 girls. If I had been meeting this group for the first time, we would have had to do a lot of work to make sure that the girls had a voice in the class. I still have to be careful, but in general the girls feel at | 110 ease, even though they are so much in the minority.

In math class, most of the kids already know what it means to have a mathematical discussion. And it's fascinating to me to have the opportunity to see how ideas develop from one year to the next.

In November we were working on division. We had just finished a few sessions in which we looked at remainders in different contexts and saw them expressed as decimals or fractions. We also considered contexts in which it made sense to round up or down to the next whole number. Now I wanted to explore an extension: situations in which there are more sharers than the number of items to be shared.

I asked the class to think about 3 kids sharing 2 candy bars. Just as the discussion began, Leo looked puzzled and recalled a conversation that we had last year. He claimed that the class reached the conclusion that we couldn't divide a larger number into a smaller number. As he presented the facts of last year's discussion, others began to nod. They were recalling the conversation and the contexts we used in our $5 \div 39$ controversy. Now they were looking at me accusingly. How could I be asking them to divide 2 candy bars among 3 kids if we already "knew" that we couldn't do it?

This situation made me wonder about the wisdom of leaving students in the middle of a misunderstanding. Would they have understood any more if last year I had told them that we *can* divide 39 into 5? Would they have been as invested in today's discussion? Were they now having an intuitive sense that we *could* do it? Although it was not my planned entry point into this new division idea—I had intended to work with easier numbers—we stuck with $5 \div 39$ because the class had an investment in it. I began by writing on the board $5 \div 39$ and $39 \div 5$.

ANTHONY: I think that $39 \div 5$ will be 7 remainder 4, but I think that $5 \div 39$ will make a decimal number.

I wonder if he is thinking of a number less than 1, and I wonder why he went to a decimal rather than a fraction. I was surprised because fractions "look" more like "less than 1" than decimals do—at least they do to me.

JACKSON: I think that you will end up with a fraction of a number because, well, because, 5 and 39—you can't divide 5 by 39 equally. I think it's going to be a number below 0.

I think that Jackson is headed in the right direction, especially when he says "a fraction *of* a number." (Am I just hoping that the number is 1?)

MaryAnn

GRADE 5, NOVEMBER

I wonder aloud about the answer being a fraction, and then about the idea that it would be below 0. I believe that if I had stuck with my original 2 ÷ 3 problem in the candy-bar context, this might have been easier to visualize. But I don't know if the students would have been so invested; they have a sense of ownership over the problems involving 5 and 39. 150

ALEJANDRO: I agree with Anthony but not with Jackson. We had some story problems where the answers were decimals but they were not below 0. I think we could say that 39 ÷ 5 could be a decimal number. [*He goes to the board and shows how he solved for a quotient of 7.8.*] I think that this is what Anthony means. 155

Anthony says that this is *not* what he means, but that he doesn't feel ready yet to explain. Alejandro used decimals to solve 39 ÷ 5, but did not try 5 ÷ 39 and did not address the crucial point of using a decimal to name a number smaller than 1. I'm pretty sure that this is where Anthony's going, but I respect his decision to remain quiet for now. 160

DARRELL: I think 39 can't go into 5. I mean, it can go into it, but it's going to be a fraction, it's got to be a fraction. A larger number into a smaller number—5 can go into 39, but there's a remainder. No, it's not a remainder; it's not a number. 165

I really don't get what Darrell is saying. Does he think that fractions or decimals are only remainders? Why does he think that it's "not a number"? 170

GREG: I agree with Anthony and with Jackson because 39 divided by 5, no, 5 divided by 39. . . .

Greg repeats the two problems four or five times. There's something that he's trying to sort out. However, the numbers removed from context clearly have little meaning for him. 175

LEO: 5 divided by 39 is going to be a smaller number. You have 39 people and 5 candies.

I stop to ask the class which one of the notations, 39 ÷ 5 or 5 ÷ 39, expresses Leo's story. I want to see if we are at least making a connection between the context and the correct notation. Most of the students didn't get that last year. 180

Mitchell chooses the correct notation and explains that the answer would be pieces of candy bars. (YES!)

MITCHELL: So, if each kid was going to get equal shares, they would have to cut the 5 candy bars into little equal pieces.

TEACHER: Can you name those equal pieces?

MITCHELL: They might be candy bars.

TEACHER: Can you name the fraction that they might be?

MITCHELL: [*After a long pause*] They wouldn't be able to do it.

DARN! We stop now to take a class poll. How many people think that you can do the problem 5 ÷ 39? How many think no, you can't? The results: yes, 13; no, 15.

After a pause, Leo says that he wants to change his no to a yes. He starts to explain that you cut each bar into 7 equal pieces, and then asks if he can go to the board. He draws circles to show the 39 people and then draws five rectangles for the 5 candy bars. He shows that partitioning 2 candy bars into sevenths will yield 14 pieces and then, without making the lines, indicates that partitioning 4 candy bars will produce 28 pieces. He pauses and sees then that the fifth candy bar will give him a total of 35 pieces. He then draws in lines to show that he has cut the last bar into 11 pieces. Now he's satisfied because he has a total of 39 pieces.

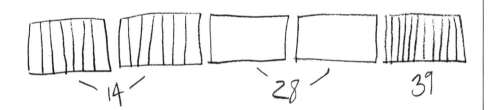

Cynthia quickly responds that this representation couldn't be correct because it isn't equal shares. She seems sure of it. There are four rectangles with sevenths and only one with elevenths. "That's a problem," she says.

As Cynthia talks, Tori goes to the board and points to the elevenths.

MaryAnn

TORI: Nobody would want one of these small pieces. There's something about Leo's solution that feels right, but something also seems wrong.   210

MARIBEL: I think that Leo is on the right track because each person would only get a really small piece, not anywhere like a whole candy bar. But Tori is right, too, because the shares that he drew aren't the same for each person.

LAILA: If I cut each of the 5 candy bars into 39 pieces and then give   215
each kid one piece from each candy bar, you could have each kid have $\frac{5}{39}$ of a candy bar.

Laila wants to go to the board and draw hers. She draws 5 rectangles divided up into 39 equal boxes. She is displaying some confidence and some clear mathematical thinking that I have not seen before.   220

ANTHONY: I think the same thing, that each person will get one piece from the first candy bar and one piece from the second and then from each one after that and will end up with 5 little pieces, so $\frac{5}{39}$.

ALEJANDRO: I was thinking that if you wanted you could take 5 from   225
each candy bar over and over again until you were done, but I think that I know that because of the drawing Laila did.

Alejandro has learned something from the discussion; Laila's work made an impact on him. I'm glad to hear him acknowledge her.

We ended the discussion right there, but continued a few days later.   230
Since I happened to have three visitors on that day (three colleagues from the professional development project I'm in), I divided the class into four groups. Each group worked with an adult to come up with a way to show $5 \div 39$. Time passed very quickly and we had little time for groups to report back to the whole class.   235

Leo and Cynthia said that they didn't really have a name for their solution, but they were ready to defend their thinking. Cynthia went to the board and drew a diagram that showed how they divided 5 candy bars for 39 people (see next page).

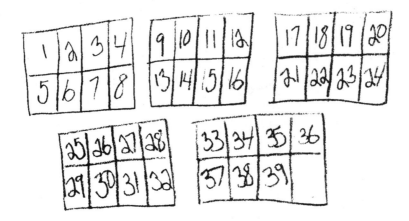

It was time to end class. Time was short and, even though all the
groups had worked hard, I think we were all feeling unsatisfied. Jackson
looked at Cynthia's diagram and asked what 40 fortieths has to do with
$5 \div 39$. I asked the students to think about that for their homework.

When we returned to the problem the next day, people were feeling
refreshed again, ready to take on Cynthia's diagram. While her drawing
helped some of the students picture the problem, it raised even more
questions:

What is the last piece called? Is it $\frac{1}{8}$ or $\frac{1}{40}$?

What's the whole?

What happens if the last piece is divided into 39 pieces? What if it is
divided into 40 pieces?

Do we know what $\frac{5}{39}$ means? Is "slightly more than $\frac{1}{8}$" a better answer
than $\frac{5}{39}$ because it's clearer, even though it's less exact? What about
$\frac{1}{8}$ and $\frac{1}{39}$ of $\frac{1}{8}$? What about $\frac{1}{8}$ and $\frac{1}{39}$ of $\frac{1}{40}$?

When we say $\frac{1}{8}$, it's $\frac{1}{8}$ of what? When we say $\frac{1}{40}$, it's $\frac{1}{40}$ of what?

If we cut the last piece into fortieths, each person gets $\frac{1}{8}$ plus $\frac{1}{40}$ of $\frac{1}{8}$.
What happens to the extra fortieth? Do we keep on dividing it? (This
is where we discussed the "piece," the "sliver," and the "crumb.")

Some of these questions I need to sort out for myself.

C H A P T E R

5

Combining shares, or adding fractions

Earlier, in chapter 2, you read cases from grades 1–3 describing children's work in whole-number addition and subtraction. In this chapter, we return to addition, but now we examine children in grades 4–7 who are working on adding fractions. What do we learn about the meaning of addition when we explore the complexities of adding fractions? What must we understand about fractions in order to figure out how to add them?

Sharing brownies or adding fractions

MaryAnn

GRADE 4, FEBRUARY

For the last two weeks, my class has been working on the *Fair Shares* unit of the curriculum *Investigations in Number, Data, and Space* (Dale Seymour, 1998). As I previewed the unit, it seemed to me that it barely scratched the surface of work with fractions. I didn't see much evidence of adding, subtracting, or multiplying with fractional numbers. Where were all the exercises in recognizing what fractional part was shaded? It looked to me like an abundance of cutting and moving around rectangles of paper, called "brownies," and lots of pleasant conversations. My initial reaction was that this was going to fall far short of my expectations for fourth graders. On the other hand, I've been using this curriculum long enough to know that my superficial preview would be buried under an avalanche of learning opportunities.

For days we cut paper brownies, shared them, rejoined fractional pieces, and discussed our brownie "fair shares." All the students were actively engaged, and for most children, understanding grew daily.

When my colleague, Janie, gave me her Problem of the Week last week, I felt that it would fit right in with what my class was doing. Each week, Janie picks a problem and distributes it to all the staff at our school—teachers, administrators, support staff, everyone. And lots of people work on it. Our staff development coordinator has declared herself "math phobic," but she works on the problem every week and is determined to learn how to solve problems like these. The custodian also submits his solution each week. Some of the teachers give the problems to their students.

Anyway, this particular problem came from *Seeing Fractions: A Unit for the Upper Elementary Grades* (California Department of Education, 1990; developed by TERC). It reads as follows:

 I invited 8 people to my party (including me) and I only had 3 brownies. How much did each person get if they had fair shares?

30

We were still hungry, and I finally found 2 more brownies in the bottom of the cookie jar. They were stale, but we ate them anyway. This time, how much did each person get?

How much brownie had each person eaten altogether?

The problem is quite a bit more complex than those we had been 35 working on. It has three parts, and the third question involves adding fractions with unlike denominators. We hadn't yet done anything like that. I don't think I would have chosen this problem on my own, but since it arrived in my mailbox, I decided to give it a try. I wondered what my students would do with it. 40

We have spent three days of math class on the problem. The children worked on their own or in pairs, as they chose, while I moved around the room holding discussions to see how they understood the problem. Sometimes, I asked the children to share their strategies with the rest of the class. Now, on this third day, I'm looking over their written work. 45

Although everybody wrote something that related to fractions, a couple of children didn't pick up on the concept of *fair shares*. They took the 3 brownies, broke them into 8 pieces, and wrote out $\frac{1}{2} + \frac{1}{2} + \frac{1}{2} + \frac{1}{2} + \frac{1}{4} + \frac{1}{4} + \frac{1}{4} + \frac{1}{4}$. They felt satisfied that this was a solution to the problem.

Most of the children did come up with a valid answer to each of the 50 three questions. I am quite interested in Maribel's work. She has devised a procedure that she applies to all cases of fair shares: Cut the brownies so that each person gets one piece from each brownie. For example, to answer the first question, she drew 8 faces for the 8 people at the party and drew 3 brownies, which she cut into eighths. She then began distrib- 55 uting the pieces to the people. Each time she distributed 8 pieces, she crossed out the brownie they came from. After she finished distributing the pieces, she counted them up. "They each get $\frac{3}{8}$," she wrote. Maribel then applied the same procedure to answer the second question, concluding, "They each get $\frac{2}{8}$." 60

Looking at Maribel's work on the first two questions (see Figure 21), I would have expected her to say something like, "If they first got $\frac{3}{8}$ and then later got $\frac{2}{8}$, that means that they got $\frac{5}{8}$ all together." But that's not what she did. Instead, she treated the third question as if it were a completely new problem: 8 people shared 5 brownies. She drew her 8 faces and drew her 5 brownies and applied the same procedure again (see Figure 22). There's certainly nothing incorrect about her procedure, and she felt satisfied with her answer of $\frac{5}{8}$. I wonder if she recognizes that she could have solved the problem by adding.

Figure 21. Maribel's work on the first two parts of the brownie-sharing problem.

Figure 22. Maribel's work on the third question in the brownie problem.

Alejandro used a method common to several other students in the class. He first saw that 2 brownies could be distributed among 8 people if you cut them into fourths, and he drew out the 8 quarter-portions. The third brownie could be cut into eighths, so for each person he drew an eighth next to the fourth. He concluded, "First they got $\frac{1}{4}$ and $\frac{1}{8}$." For the second part of the problem, he again distributed the 2 brownies by cutting them into fourths, drawing in another quarter-portion for each person: "Then they got $\frac{1}{4}$." Looking at his pictorial representation,

70

75

Chapter 5

87

Alejandro concluded, "Altogether they got $\frac{2}{4}$ and $\frac{1}{8}$." He also drew
a brownie and shaded in $\frac{1}{4}$ and $\frac{1}{4}$ and $\frac{1}{8}$ (see Figure 23).

80

I feel quite satisfied with the work of the children who solved the
problem the way Alejandro did, but I still have questions about what they
are thinking. In the brownie at the lower right of Alejandro's page, which
he divided into 8 eighths, each of the parts labeled $\frac{1}{4}$ pretty clearly show
$\frac{2}{8}$. Can he look at his drawing and see that $\frac{1}{4} = \frac{2}{8}$? Can he see that he has
shaded in $\frac{5}{8}$? Does he see that, when Maribel says each person got $\frac{5}{8}$ of a
brownie, her answer represents the same amount as his? I expect to have
opportunities in the coming days to follow up these questions about what
my students are thinking.

85

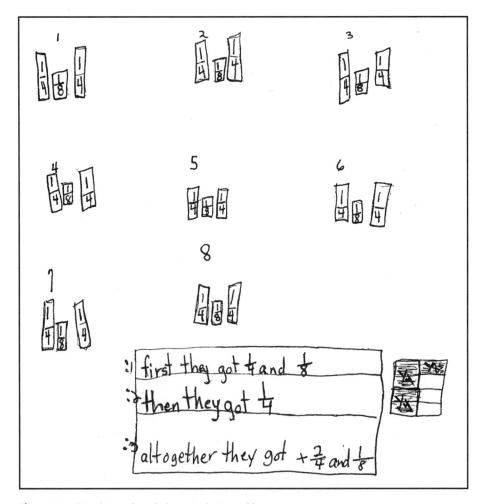

Figure 23. Alejandro's work on the brownie-sharing problem.

Usually I distribute my time pretty evenly among my students, asking them questions while they are working. Sometimes, however, I give more of my time to children who especially need attention; then I catch up with the others later. During the three days that we worked on this problem, I spent much of my time with Jackson.

Jackson is a sweet kid who is almost always disorganized. At the beginning of the school year, I found it hard to listen to him; he always seemed to be rambling, and it was difficult to make sense of what he was saying. His classmates seemed to have the same reaction. However, in recent years I have learned to listen hard for the ideas my students are trying to express, and when I persevered, I found that listening to Jackson offered unexpected rewards. He has good mathematical insights. And when I listen hard and take seriously what Jackson is saying, so do his classmates. Their relationship to him has improved since September.

On the day that I handed out the problem, I moved through the classroom, looking over children's shoulders, pausing to listen to their conversations, sometimes asking them questions so that I could better understand what they were thinking. By the time I got to Jackson, he had answers for all three questions. However, his page was so messy, I couldn't interpret what he had done (see Figure 24). When I asked him to explain, he could share some confident and correct thinking. Yet, as he tried to retrace what he had done, he lost track of his thinking and couldn't make sense of his own disorganized written work.

For the first question, Jackson was able to explain quickly that 3 brownies had been cut up so that 8 people each received $\frac{1}{4}$ from the first two brownies and then each received $\frac{1}{8}$ from the third. He noted that each fair share was $\frac{1}{4} + \frac{1}{8}$. (Unlike Alejandro, Jackson used the plus sign instead of the word *and*.)

Jackson's illustration for the second question showed 2 brownies cut into 8 equal shares of $\frac{1}{4}$ each. His answer to the second question was $\frac{1}{4}$.

The third part got very messy. Unfortunately for Jackson, much good thinking gets lost because of his poor organizational skills. It was difficult for him to figure out what he had done in this section. He knew what the question was, but he seemed to feel that he had to reconstruct the whole problem before he could reach a conclusion. (This is what Maribel had done, too.) I wonder why he didn't realize that he had already figured out much of what he needed to know, and that he just needed to use the information from the first two parts.

When Jackson worked to distribute 5 brownies among 8 people, he figured that they got $\frac{1}{4}$ and $\frac{1}{4}$ and $\frac{1}{8}$. We can see on his paper that he wrote $\frac{1}{4} + \frac{1}{4} + \frac{1}{8}$ in a vertical column and came up with an answer of $\frac{3}{8}$.

At this point, it appeared that Jackson had separated the numbers from the problem context. When I asked him how he got $\frac{3}{8}$, he explained that he added the 1s (the numerators) and then added $4 + 4$, two of the denominators, to get 8. He decided that since the other denominator is also 8, it stays the same, "So $\frac{3}{8}$." Jackson wanted to be satisfied with this answer and wanted me to leave him alone. Instead, I asked him to think about the third part of the problem and told him we'd talk about it again later. This was the end of the first day.

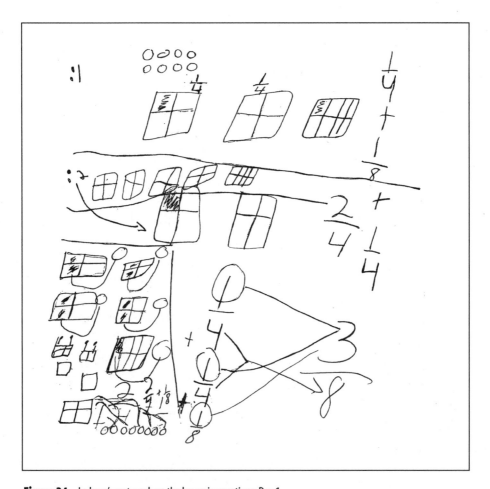

Figure 24. Jackson's seat work on the brownie questions, Day 1.

Figure 25. Jackson's board work explaining his solution to the brownie problem, Day 2.

The next day I had some of the children share their solutions on the board. Jackson came to the board to talk about the third question (see Figure 25).

JACKSON: All right, draw 5 brownies, like this. [*He draws 5 squares.*] Cut the first two into 4 parts each [*which he does*], and then make the next one into 8 parts. [*Without speaking, he also divides the last two squares into eighths.*]

Although I knew that this would work out OK, I wondered aloud why he had changed his strategy from yesterday's attempt. He shrugged. Then he counted up what each person got and came up with an answer of $\frac{1}{4}$ and $\frac{3}{8}$. This time he didn't try to combine them to create a single fractional number.

I was struck by the clarity of Jackson's presentation. Although he frequently loses focus when working with complex problems, once focused, he can confidently arrive at an accurate solution.

However, our work on the problem—and my thinking about Jackson—wasn't done. The next day, we continued the group discussion about the children's various solutions. When one child said that he didn't understand what Jackson had done, Jackson offered to explain it again, one-on-one. I was interested to hear how he would rephrase the problem and his solution, so I listened in.

Chapter 5

Figure 26. Jackson's attempt to explain his solution to a classmate, Day 3.

Jackson showed how the first 3 brownies could be distributed among 8 people to make portions of $\frac{1}{4} + \frac{1}{8}$ (see Figure 26). He then showed how the next 2 brownies would give each person $\frac{1}{4}$. I noted that he had gone back to his original strategy. And then, in a change from his first-day approach, Jackson began to work on the third question without redoing the entire problem; he seemed to realize that the answer could be derived from the first two parts. However, he did come up with the same answer: $\frac{1}{4} + \frac{1}{4} + \frac{1}{8} = \frac{3}{8}$. I wanted to hear more.

TEACHER: I see that you did some work with the fractions over here. [*I point to some crossed-out figures on his paper.*] I'm wondering why you crossed out some numbers.

JACKSON: I was adding the 1 + 1 + 1 and it came to 3, but then I went to add the bottoms [4 + 4 + 8] and it didn't make sense. There's nothing here that's 16, and the numbers I was getting wouldn't match the brownies. When I looked at the brownies, I could see that each person had $\frac{1}{4}$ and $\frac{1}{4}$ and $\frac{1}{8}$, and I know the $\frac{1}{4}$ and $\frac{1}{4}$ make $\frac{1}{2}$, and then $\frac{1}{8}$. So, I'm telling you each person had a share of $\frac{1}{2}$ and $\frac{1}{8}$.

It turns out that when Jackson tried to add, he wasn't simply looking at the numerals without considering the problem context. After all, he rejected $\frac{3}{16}$ as an answer—it didn't make sense in this context. So he manipulated the symbols in a different way and came up with an answer, $\frac{3}{8}$, that seemed more reasonable to him.

Jackson had come up with three different correct representations for a single fair share in this problem:

$$\frac{1}{4} + \frac{1}{4} + \frac{1}{8} \qquad \frac{1}{4} \text{ and } \frac{3}{8} \qquad \frac{1}{2} \text{ and } \frac{1}{8}$$

I wonder how he perceives Alejandro's $\frac{2}{4}$ and $\frac{1}{8}$, or Maribel's answer of $\frac{5}{8}$.

Up ahead for all my students is the work of sorting out the ideas behind adding fractions with unlike denominators. I'll be watching how they think this through, building on the ideas they already have in place.

C A S E **21**

How many ways can you add 1/3 to 1/4? Or, interesting stuff happens!

Henry

GRADE 6, DECEMBER

This year I teach sixth-grade math to three different groups each day. I have found that the more control I assume and structure I apply, the more similar the three classes will be on a given day. When I give up some of that control and allow the students to determine more of the agenda, those groups move in wildly divergent directions.

A recent lesson looked quite simple in my plan book. We had been adding fractions with like denominators and had begun to get ready to deal with unlike denominators. We had experimented with finding common multiples, explored equivalency, practiced simplifying fractions, and begun changing fractions to higher terms.

I was feeling that we were in the thick of a computational jungle, and I wanted us to look at some concepts together. I also wanted to get an idea of what my students were thinking. For my lesson, I asked the students to make pictures (diagrams) of what is happening when we add $\frac{1}{3}$ to $\frac{1}{4}$. Each class handled it very differently.

In the first class, I started out by asking the group to draw what happens when we add $\frac{1}{3}$ to $\frac{1}{3}$. Alexandra came to the board to show us her picture. She drew it out this way:

first $\frac{1}{3}$	first $\frac{1}{3}$	
$\frac{1}{3}$	$\frac{1}{3}$	

Making Meaning for Operations

This seemed quite straightforward; no one offered a different notion or any objections. Thinking that this was just how I saw it, I plowed forward with the main lesson, asking the class to work in groups to draw a picture of $\frac{1}{3} + \frac{1}{4}$. (There were a few other instructions, too, such as create a story problem to accompany the numbers, and explain your group's picture and approach to another group, but for this case I am focusing on the pictures they drew.)

All groups used Alexandra's work as a model, and although there were certainly some moments of struggle, groups produced this type of drawing:

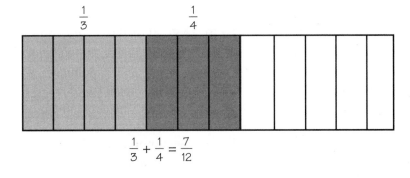

$$\frac{1}{3} + \frac{1}{4} = \frac{7}{12}$$

When asked how exactly they came up with the twelfths, they answered that they "found a common denominator and changed to higher terms" and so on. In other words, they mimicked the computation we had been doing in the previous days and did not look beneath the computational surface of the problem. It wasn't really their fault either, for this is sort of what I expected, what I wanted. This was an obvious reaction to what I had set up.

The second class began with the same instructions; however, our model student, Ramón, opened up a mathematical Pandora's Box with his drawing of $\frac{1}{3} + \frac{1}{3}$:

He explained this to be equal to $\frac{2}{3}$, but Tanya wondered, "Isn't that really equal to 2 out of 6 or $\frac{2}{6}$, which is just $\frac{1}{3}$? But how could $\frac{1}{3} + \frac{1}{3} = \frac{1}{3}$?"

In trying to sort this out, Colin came up with this example:

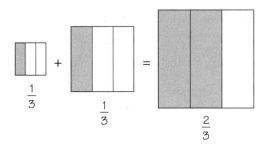

Of course the different-sized wholes then brought up other issues. Ten minutes into this lesson I had discovered that a good deal of confusion lived just beneath the surface—not the computational surface, but the conceptual one. I know that it was there in the first class, too, but I just wasn't able to get it to bubble up.

For the third class, I completely abandoned my preconceived plans and expectations. I decided to do away with the model example of $\frac{1}{3} + \frac{1}{3}$ and to start with $\frac{1}{3} + \frac{1}{4}$. I asked the students to try not to think about any computational angles, but to attempt to picture their understandings. This approach yielded entirely different results. Lizette showed this diagram to get started on $\frac{1}{3} + \frac{1}{4}$:

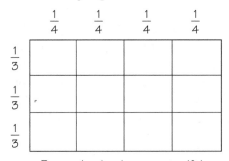

3 rows by 4 columns = twelfths

We began to investigate if this type of picture would be a good way to come up with a lowest common multiple for two numbers. The conversations and investigations were lively. In the midst of it all, some kids were doing exactly what I do when I am involved in similar situations as a student. They were "doing their own thing," going off on tangents, discovering ideas that have been experienced by others millions of times

230

235

240

245

but that were new to them. Why didn't this environment exist in the other two classes? I wondered and still wonder. I'm sure that much of the answer is that I did not allow it to exist, or, to put it more mildly, I did not effectively sponsor it.

250

As this class ended, one student, Ming-hua, came up to tell me that he had discovered something cool:

$$\begin{array}{c} \dfrac{1}{3} \\ + \dfrac{1}{4} \\ \hline \dfrac{7}{12} \end{array} \quad \text{because it's} \quad \dfrac{3+4}{3\times 4} \qquad\qquad \begin{array}{c} \dfrac{1}{15} \\ + \dfrac{1}{2} \\ \hline \dfrac{17}{30} \end{array} \quad \text{because it's} \quad \dfrac{15+2}{15\times 2}$$

My reaction to Ming-hua? "WOW!"

In conclusion, what does it all mean? Honestly, I'm not sure. I know that does not establish closure, so . . . I guess it means that the teacher sets the tone for the lesson and the environment of the class—consciously, but often times unconsciously, too. When I don't expect my students to be clones of me and merely follow my lead, when I genuinely listen to their questions and don't rush to answer them, interesting stuff happens.

255

C A S E **22**

"Doling out" and fractions

Greta

GRADES 6 AND 7 (SPECIAL ED), NOVEMBER

I have been thinking about how my students use "doling" as a strategy for solving fraction problems of this type: division of whole numbers with the remainder expressed as a fraction. The strategy of doling out has its pros and cons. On the upside, doling is very systematic and easy to understand. On the downside, some of my students can't reassemble all

260

Greta

the fractional pieces into just one fraction. For others the equivalency issue is akin to changing the problem.

For example, consider one boy's approach to this problem:

? 4 kids share 19 pizzas. How much will each kid get?

Gunther will dole out all the wholes first: The 4 kids each get 4 whole pizzas. Then taking the 3 remaining pies, he will cut 2 of them in half, dole out each $\frac{1}{2}$, then cut the last pie in 4 pieces and dole out $\frac{1}{4}$ to each kid. Gunther writes as his answer: "The first boy gets 4 wholes and a half and $\frac{1}{4}$. The second boy gets 4 wholes and a half and $\frac{1}{4}$. The third boy gets . . . ." Gunther is very systematic in breaking down the pizza into ever smaller pieces. But when Mercedes says that her answer, $4\frac{3}{4}$, is the same as his, he initially objects. She shows him how his half pieces can be cut into fourths. "But I know I got the answer; this changes my drawing," he protests. There are two underlying issues for him, I think: He doesn't yet know that mixed numbers are conventionally expressed as a whole and one fraction, and that fractional pieces like $\frac{1}{2}$ and $\frac{1}{4}$ can be added.

Another boy handled the following problem in an interesting way:

? 3 kids share one stick of gum. How much does each get?

Dominic wrote:

$\frac{4}{4}$ equals 1 whole. So we divide it into four parts: $\frac{1}{4}$ $\frac{2}{4}$ $\frac{3}{4}$ $\frac{4}{4}$. Each kid is going to get $\frac{1}{4}$. So $\frac{3}{4}$ are gone. [There] is $\frac{1}{4}$ left so we need to divide $\frac{1}{4}$ into $\frac{1}{12}$ pieces. [Each kid gets] $\frac{1}{4}$ and $\frac{1}{12}$.

Dominic's drawing looked first as shown at left; then he extended the three horizontal lines to make twelfths.

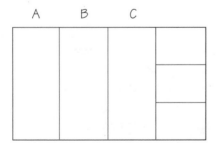

265

270

275

280

285

Making Meaning for Operations

While showing and describing his work, Dominic realized that $\frac{1}{4}$ and $\frac{1}{12}$ could also be called $\frac{4}{12}$. When I asked if there was an easier way to do this problem, Dominic returned with a drawing showing thirds:

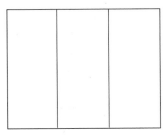

Dominic, like Gunther, would have left his answer as $\frac{1}{4} + \frac{1}{12}$, except that our conversation about his drawing led him to the other answer. Again I started thinking about how students sometimes shy away from combining fractional pieces on the initial solution.

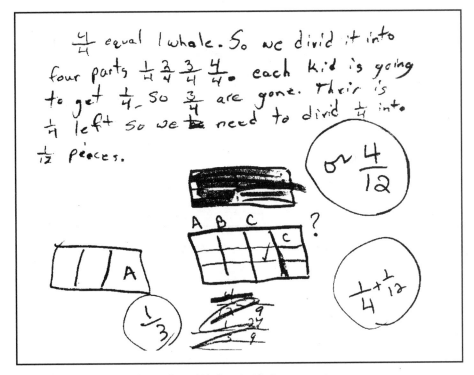

Figure 27. Dominic's work showing how 3 kids share 1 stick of gum.

Greta

GRADES 6 AND 7 (SPECIAL ED), NOVEMBER

In another problem of this type, 9 kids shared 21 pizzas. How much did each get? For this problem, some students chose to use small plastic circles to represent the pizzas. Antonio was able to dole out 2 wholes for each of the 9 kids. Then on the "leftover" 3 circles, he drew lines on the plastic and numbered 9 slices. When asked about his work, Antonio explained that each kid got 2 wholes and $\frac{1}{9}$ and $\frac{1}{9}$ and $\frac{1}{9}$. However, while he worked on recording his ideas on paper (Figure 28), he forgot how many ninths each kid got and gave 2 and $\frac{1}{9}$ as his answer.

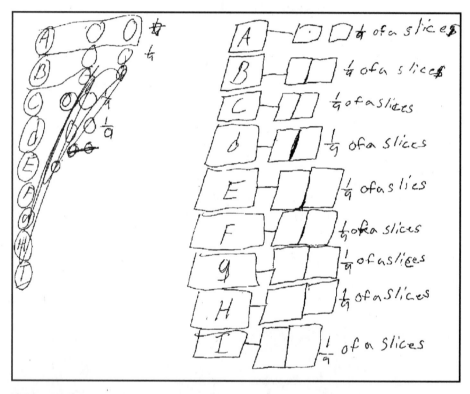

Figure 28. After first using plastic circles to solve the sharing of 9 pizzas among 21 kids, Antonio tried to represent his work on paper.

Making Meaning for Operations

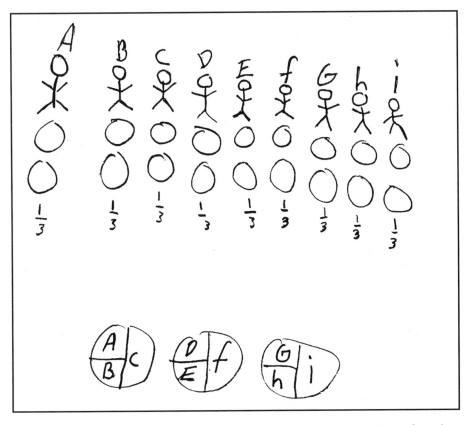

Figure 29. In Zoe's work, showing her solution to 9 kids sharing 21 pizzas, she doles out 18 pizzas first and divides the leftover 3 into thirds.

On the same problem Zoe showed an impressive ability to keep straight in her head a lot of information. She laid out 36 plastic circles in a 9-by-4 array. I thought that she was totally confused. She proved me wrong. She told me the first row across was the 9 kids. The next 2 rows were the wholes. The bottom row was the thirds. I was amazed since all the circles were identical. When she worked on paper (as shown in Figure 29), Zoe represented the kids, whole pizzas, and thirds differently. That was less confusing for me.

305

310

C H A P T E R

6

Taking portions of portions, or multiplying fractions

In chapter 3 of this casebook, Linda wrote, "As we turned away from our intense study of subtraction, I was curious to find out what my fourth graders knew about multiplication. What did they think it was? How was it different from the operations we had just been studying? These were questions I had been thinking about for myself as well as for my students, and I hadn't come to any solid conclusions yet."

At the time, we considered Linda's questions in the context of whole numbers. How do our answers change now, in the realm of fractions? What type of situations could be modeled by, say, $\frac{1}{3} \times \frac{1}{4}$, and what is it about such

103

situations that make multiplication appropriate? How do we think about multiplication when the numbers in the problem already have division implied in them?

A fourth into three parts: One thirty-twoth?

Georgia

GRADES 3 AND 4, DECEMBER

All year I have wondered whether doing a lot of division would help my students think about fractions. While watching them work division problems, I've seen them add, subtract, and multiply. What does this tell me about the way they think about division and, most recently, fractions? Although many of them talk about fractions or give fractions as answers, I have not formally taught fractions this year. I have been intrigued by how well kids think about fractions without manipulatives or specific instruction. They are intuitive and capable in this area of math.

The other day I overheard two girls talking about what half of a half is. I wasn't clear how the conversation had started, but I asked if I could join them and take notes on what they said. They were excited to share their thinking, so we had an impromptu math group. They were both convinced that the answer to half of a half was a "quarter." They went on to explain their thinking.

JUSTINE: It would be split into 4 pieces. It's already into 2 pieces, and then if you split it into 4 pieces, then you make each half in half.

CASSANDRA: You have 2 halves and then you split only 1 in half. Then you have 2 quarters and 1 half. [*She draws a picture.*]

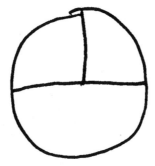

| JUSTINE: | But what I mean is, if you split both halves in half, then you'd have quarters. | 20 |

I was interested in how they each were thinking about the whole. Why had Justine divided the whole into 4 pieces while Cassandra took only a half to divide in half? How was Cassandra able to think about quarters or fourths without actually having 4 pieces? She didn't need to see the whole thing. I asked them if we needed to split both halves in half.

| JUSTINE: | Yes, because then it would be even. |

| CASSANDRA: | You didn't say there were 2 halves, you said 1, and half of a half is a quarter, and 4 quarters make a whole. |

| JUSTINE: | That's the same as I did it. |

At this point I thought that both girls just knew the answer. The whole was implicit in their understanding of the problem, so I tried to make up a question that was similar to the one we began with. I then asked them what a half of a quarter was. They answered quickly, "An eighth."

| JUSTINE: | I think I've done fractions before because I know when you split something in half it's twice as much—and then I wasn't sure so I checked it by doing what Cassandra did. [*They both have drawn a picture.*] And if you did eighths in half it would be sixteenths and so on. [*Both girls laugh and in unison say, "Then thirty-twoths, and sixty-fourths."*] |

CASSANDRA: Because what I did was make a whole, and then I split it into quarters, and then I split each quarter in half. Then I counted how many triangles, and there were 8, so I knew it was an eighth. You see there was 1 circle with 8 pieces—the 1 refers to the circle and the 8 refers to the pieces—so $\frac{1}{8}$. 45

JUSTINE: No. The 1 doesn't refer to the whole round thing. It talks about the . . . [*She stops and draws a picture.*] They're talking about 1 of these eighths, and if it were 2 eighths, it would be this:

So, if you divide a fourth into 3 parts, it is 1 thirty-twoth, I think. 50

CASSANDRA: I get it. If there were 8 pieces and you colored in 1 and then you counted all of them—which is 8—it would be 1 eighth.

I wondered how Justine got $\frac{1}{32}$. On reflection, I now think she doubled the denominator of $\frac{1}{4}$ and got $\frac{1}{8}$, then doubled again to get $\frac{1}{16}$, and 55 doubled for a third time to get $\frac{1}{32}$. At the time I wasn't clear about this, so I asked them to look at the problem that Justine had posed. "What does 1 fourth divided into 3 parts look like? Can you come up with a math sentence?" By this point, Austin had wandered over to join the math group, and he spoke up. 60

AUSTIN: I think it's a sixteenth, because if you take a fourth and you split it into 4 pieces—if you split it in half, it's an eighth, and then in half again, it's an 8, and then you have to add 4. So it's a twelfth. [*He drew this picture.*]

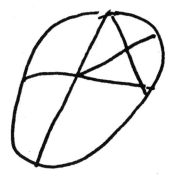

Cassandra said she was confused, but Justine, who had been ready to   65
burst ever since Austin showed up, jumped in.

JUSTINE: It's 4 times 3 which is 12, of course. OK, this is how it goes:
            You have a circle thing. You have a fourth and you cut it into
            3 pieces. Then I cut it all into 3 pieces.

This is what she drew: 70

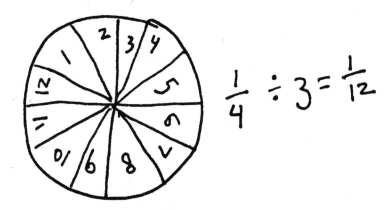

She added, "It's not 12 somethings. It's $\frac{1}{12}$."

I have a few random thoughts about this episode. I don't feel any
closer to knowing whether our work with division has been helpful to the
children in thinking about fractions, but I do know that I feel more
informed about how my students approach division. Many begin their   75
work with fractions and division by splitting numbers in half or

doubling. In previous experiences, I have found children's fraction drawings to get messy and confusing. In this session, the drawings were helpful. What was the difference? Are drawings helpful only when children are clear about their thinking? Do children have to be at a certain place in their understanding of fractions for drawings to be helpful? When you "double" fractions (double the denominator, that is), is it easier to draw and consequently clearer?

C A S E **24**

Clock faces and equivalence

Ann

GRADE 6, NOVEMBER

As my sixth-grade students explored equivalent fractions, I used a lesson from TERC's *Investigations,* in the *Name That Portion* unit. It asked the students to look at clock faces and determine what portion of the clock face the hour hand has passed through since 12 o'clock (see Figure 30). I have come to expect the unexpected when conducting a math lesson, and this lesson was no exception.

Jaclyn started with the clock reading 1 o'clock. "I think it's $\frac{1}{12}$ because there are 12 parts and 1 of them is being used."

Rusty chimed in, "It could be a $\frac{5}{60}$, too, because there are 60 minutes in an hour and 5 minutes are the portion shown."

Midori suggested, "It could be $\frac{2}{24}$ because that is equal to $\frac{1}{12}$."

"What portion would $\frac{1}{24}$ represent on the clock?" I asked.

Liam raised his hand. "It would be $2\frac{1}{2}$ minutes, because $\frac{2}{24}$ is 5 minutes, so half of 5 minutes is $2\frac{1}{2}$ minutes."

I asked if there were any other ideas, and Amini spoke up: "It could also be $\frac{1}{3}$ of $\frac{1}{4}$ of the clock face."

This response initially brought puzzled looks and questions to the other students and to me. What was Amini seeing? First he was looking at the whole clock face and breaking it into quarters, then looking at just

Figure 30. From the Clock Fractions handout in *Name That Portion*, a grade 5 unit of *Investigations in Number, Data, and Space®*, © 1998 by Dale Seymour Publications.

the one quarter, he noticed that a third of it was the portion marked. This ability to look at a portion of a portion was unexpected.

As we looked at the other clock faces, students continued to point out this portion-of-a-portion equivalency. Ferris said that the clock face showing 2 o'clock was $\frac{2}{3}$ of $\frac{1}{4}$. For 3 o'clock, Liam said the portion shown was $\frac{1}{6}$

105

plus $\frac{1}{2}$ of $\frac{1}{6}$. Ferris suggested that we could also call it $\frac{1}{2}$ of $\frac{1}{2}$. Midori saw 4 o'clock as $\frac{4}{6}$ of $\frac{1}{2}$. Similar examples happened on each clock face.

Not all students were able to see these equivalencies. What is necessary for a student—or a teacher—to see them? I speculate that one must be able to identify the whole first. In this case, the clock face was the whole. After recognizing this, you have to notice a portion of the whole, such as $\frac{1}{2}$ or $\frac{1}{4}$, and have *this* become the "whole" you focus on for a while—but you still need to hold onto its relationship with the whole clock face. You then compare the new whole ($\frac{1}{2}$ or $\frac{1}{4}$, for example) to the portion indicated by the hour hand. Is the hour hand's movement a sixth of the new portion, a half of it, a third of it? To do this, someone must be able to see relationships within relationships. I feel that this is a big mathematical issue for my students.

C A S E   **25**

Multiplication of mixed numbers

Sarita

I asked the students in my sixth-grade class to solve the following problem by drawing a large, clearly labeled picture:

? What is the area of a rectangle that has a width of $2\frac{3}{4}$ and a length of $3\frac{2}{3}$?

As I was walking around the classroom, listening to and observing students working on the problem, I overheard the following comment:

YURI: Usually all you have to do to find the area is to multiply the length times the width, but because we have fractions, you can't do that.

We had spent many weeks working on area and perimeter problems, so the students were familiar with finding the area of a region by counting the number of units or, in the case of rectangles, by multiplying the width times the length. Why did Yuri think this method would not apply with fractions?

When we started the whole-group discussion, Olivia volunteered to come to the board and discuss her strategy for solving the problem. She carefully drew her picture on the board.

$$3\frac{2}{3}$$

$$2\frac{3}{4}$$

OLIVIA:	You can get some of the area but not all of it.
TEACHER:	What part of the area can you get?
OLIVIA:	I know that the length times the width is the area, so $2 \times 3 = 6$.
TEACHER:	Where is the 2×3, or the 6, in the picture?
OLIVIA:	The big squares are the wholes and you can just count 6. The smaller pieces you can count, too, but they don't count as wholes.
TEACHER:	Why not?

OLIVIA: Those pieces aren't whole squares the way that the other ones are, because of the fractions. So [*counting to herself*], there are 4 of those [*she points to the rectangles at the top right*], and that is $1\frac{1}{3}$. If you put 4 fourths together, that's 2 wholes and $\frac{1}{4}$ left. But I don't know how to count the other pieces.

150

TEACHER: Why not?

OLIVIA: They are like pieces of pieces of something.

KYLE: Like fractions of pieces when the pieces are fractions.

There was a pause in the class as they mulled that one over. Then there was a flutter of voices as the children talked to one another. I let them discuss this for a minute or two.

155

TEACHER: Can someone paraphrase what Kyle said?

SHANTEA: I think he is saying that those pieces are fractions of fractions, but what is that anyway?

160

MERYL: There is $\frac{2}{3}$ on one side and $\frac{3}{4}$ on the other side.

GERALDO: Almost like $\frac{2}{3}$ of $\frac{3}{4}$, but that's not possible.

CECILIA: Yeah! No way could you have $\frac{2}{3}$ of $\frac{3}{4}$!

At this point I decided to introduce an idea that might ease the struggle that the students were having. I used the example that Geraldo and another student had posed, but I put the idea into a simple and meaningful context.

165

TEACHER: Think about this. Someone gave me $\frac{3}{4}$ of a leftover candy bar. [*I draw a diagram on the board.*]

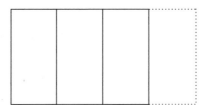

I ate $\frac{2}{3}$ of that for lunch. What part of the whole candy bar did I eat? | 170

MAURICE: Two thirds of $\frac{3}{4}$. That's got to be $\frac{6}{12}$. Just put some lines here, and you can see the $\frac{6}{12}$. [*He adds two horizontal lines to my diagram and shades in a portion showing $\frac{2}{3}$ of $\frac{3}{4}$.*] And $\frac{6}{12}$ is the same as $\frac{1}{2}$. | 175

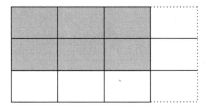

FELICIA: He's right!

Mario said he saw the $\frac{2}{3}$ as two of the three pieces of the leftover candy bar (in the original diagram), which he could then see was half of the whole candy bar.

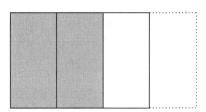

Students discussed this information until the idea was more comfortable for them. They returned to the original problem and decided that we could indeed find the area of the entire region by taking all the things that we had counted and adding them together. They added unlike denominators by using Olivia's picture and thinking about equivalent fractions as they worked through the numbers. | 180 | 185

At the end of class, Basimah was busy studying Olivia's picture on the board.

BASIMAH: You know, another way to look at this would be to extend the picture, to show the missing parts of the pieces of pieces. That way we could just see what they were. [*She extended the original diagram as she had proposed.*] Then you know that the pieces are twelfths, and you can count them the way you can count the rest of the pieces.

190

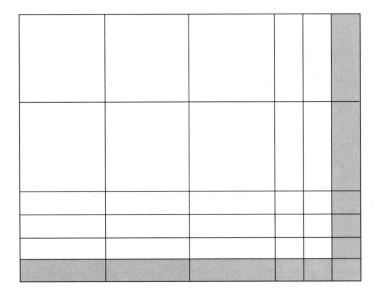

She was absolutely right! I asked her why she hadn't shared that with the class, and she said that she just now discovered it by looking at the picture.

195

After class, I reflected on the students' method to solve the problem I had posed. My goal is that the students, at some point, will develop an arithmetic algorithm from their picture. When I examine the diagram, I recognize a procedure based on partial products, much like the basic principle that underlies most common algorithms for multiplying multi-digit whole numbers.

200

To multiply $2\frac{3}{4} \times 3\frac{2}{3}$, find the partial products:

$2 \times 3 = 6$

$2 \times \frac{2}{3} = \frac{4}{3} = 1\frac{1}{3}$

205

$3 \times \frac{3}{4} = \frac{9}{4} = 2\frac{1}{4}$

$\frac{2}{3} \times \frac{3}{4} = \frac{6}{12}$

Making Meaning for Operations

Then add all the parts:

$$6 + 1\frac{1}{3} + 2\frac{1}{4} + \frac{6}{12} = 10\frac{1}{12}$$

This works, and seems very clear. But the procedure presented in most middle-grade mathematics texts involves changing mixed numbers to improper fractions, multiplying, and then changing the answer back to a mixed number.

$$2\frac{3}{4} \times 3\frac{2}{3} =$$

$$\frac{11}{4} \times \frac{11}{3} =$$

$$\frac{121}{12} = 10\frac{1}{2}$$

When I looked for these numbers in the picture, I found them by drawing more lines so that I could transform everything into fourths and thirds. By making darker lines to keep straight what stood for 1, I could then see how the twelfths appear.

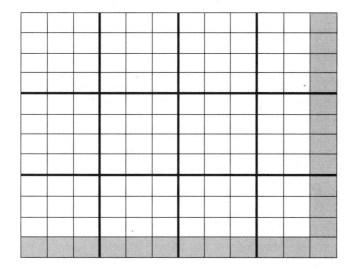

Now that I understand this better for myself, I still need to think through my goals for my students.

What I want my students to understand about multiplication

Henry
GRADE 6, DECEMBER

"What is it you want your students to understand?" has been asked of me so often over the two years that I've been in this professional development project, I now automatically ask the question of myself. This represents a change, because I used to set my goals by thinking "these are the things I want my students to be able to *do*"—not unlike trained seals. My students could move numbers around and about; understanding was expected to come as part of the package. However, I'm not sure I ever knew exactly what I wanted them to understand. This is my attempt to nail down a few ideas about multiplication.

1. *Multiplication does not always make things bigger.*

   Whole-number multiplication leaves students with some observations and assumptions that do not hold water when decimals and fractions float by. This is one big misconception.

2. *Multiplication is not just repeated addition.*

   The link between multiplication and addition seemed to make great sense with whole-number problems, but multiplication is a great deal more complex than this.

3. *What is the mystery of "times"?*

   Many of my students read 7×9 as "7 times 9" but have no idea what that means. *Times* seems to be an unfathomable word to some of them.

4. *3 × 4 = 4 × 3, but are they the same?*

So many of my students seem "answer-driven," and the notion that multiplication is commutative makes good and easy sense to them. But 3 groups of 4 *is* different from 4 groups of 3.

{ o o o o }   { o o o }
{ o o o o }   { o o o }
{ o o o o }   { o o o }
               { o o o }

5. *How do you translate a multiplication expression, and can you understand what it means?*

The expression 5×6 could be 5 groups of 6, or it could be 5 taken 6 times. This interchangeable nature stretches a bit too far when students attempt to make sense of $\frac{1}{2} \times \frac{1}{4}$. The idea of " $\frac{1}{2}$, taken $\frac{1}{4}$ of a time" is of little value. Thinking about " $\frac{1}{2}$ group of $\frac{1}{4}$" makes better sense, but this, too, is not easy to understand. Drawings and pictures can greatly help understanding, at least when they aren't causing more confusion. My sense is that confusion in these areas—translating the multiplication equation into something understandable, and being able to represent that understanding in a picture form—is desirable, for without that confusion, students will not achieve that understanding. And I think that understanding this stuff is key to understanding multiplication itself.

6. *The numbers in a multiplication equation are connected to real things.*

I want my students to be aware that numbers don't always exist by themselves—they are useful representations of things, such as people, money, or objects. And they help us solve real-world problems. I have found that when students make the connection between realistic problems and multiplication equations, the operation of multiplication becomes clearer, and many of the misconceptions that exist when dealing only with numbers pose no threat.

7. *Students should not be hypnotized by numbers.*

A student will work with a problem like $3\frac{1}{2} \times 3\frac{1}{2}$ and get an answer such as 37, or perhaps $2\frac{1}{4}$. These answers are outrageously incorrect, but many times we become blinded while computing numbers and fail to think about what those numbers mean. I want my students to realize that $3\frac{1}{2} \times 3\frac{1}{2}$ can't possibly equal more than 4×4 or less than 3×3. Estimation is a useful tool.

Chapter 6

Henry

8. There is a real connection between multiplication and division. 275

Students seem to recite automatically that multiplication and division are opposites, and leave it at that. But to truly understand that $10 \times \frac{1}{2} = 10 \div 2$ and to contend with other problems like this, it seems necessary to dig a little deeper. And there's mathematical gold to be found here, for stuff like reciprocals and division of fractions can then been seen in a 280 different way.

Since I am sure there are more important ideas about multiplication that I have not yet touched on, I will leave this unfinished.

Making Meaning for Operations

C H A P T E R

7

Expanding ideas about division in the context of fractions

The cases in chapter 7 present the work of two sixth-grade classes as they solve problems that their teachers identify as division of fractions. These cases provide us an opportunity to study division of fractions for ourselves, but they also return us to the themes of this seminar:

- What does it mean to model a situation with a piece of arithmetic?

- As we see the various number sentences that could represent a single situation, what do we learn about the operations?

- How are our ideas about the operations extended as we encounter new situations they might model?

Who says that's not the right equation? My own experience vs. students' thinking

Sarita

GRADE 6, MAY

The students in my sixth-grade class have been solving fraction word problems for several weeks. Today they were spread around the classroom, working in groups of twos and threes. The directions were to draw a picture to solve the problem, write a number sentence (equation) that explains the problem, and show any computation. This was the problem I gave them to solve:

> **?** You are giving a birthday party. From Ben and Jerry's ice cream factory, you order 6 pints of ice cream. If you serve $\frac{3}{4}$ of a pint of ice cream to each guest, how many guests can be served?

For the most part, the students didn't find this a difficult problem. They drew pictures to represent the pints of ice cream and separated each pint into 4 equal sections. They explained that every 3 sections was what one person would receive, and that was equal to $\frac{3}{4}$. There was enough to do that 8 times, so each variety would serve 8 people.

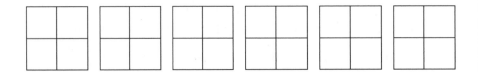

However, when they expressed this problem in a number sentence or equation, the range of answers was interesting. I use the word *interesting* because I am not sure whether the students are incorrect or whether they just see things differently. Although I could understand the thinking behind their equations, I didn't think that they were "correct." I had been taught that equations have to match what is going on in the problem. In my mind the students' equations were, though not necessarily wrong, not quite correct, either.

I was trying to get the students to see that this was a division problem: $6 \div \frac{3}{4} = 8$. Instead, they came up with the following equations and had impressive reasoning to justify their thinking:

Equation	Justification
$24 \div 3 = 8$	There are 24 pieces, 3 pieces to a serving, 8 people can be served.
$8 \times \frac{3}{4} = 6$	8 servings of $\frac{3}{4}$ of a pint each gives you 6 whole pints.
$\frac{3}{4} + \frac{3}{4} + \frac{3}{4} + \frac{3}{4} +$ $\frac{3}{4} + \frac{3}{4} + \frac{3}{4} + \frac{3}{4} = 6$	$\frac{3}{4}$ each gives you 6 whole pints.
$6 - \frac{3}{4} - \frac{3}{4} - \frac{3}{4} - \frac{3}{4} -$ $\frac{3}{4} - \frac{3}{4} - \frac{3}{4} - \frac{3}{4} = 0$	Take $\frac{3}{4}$ pint for each serving. You can do this 8 times.

Students also presented some other equations along with those listed above. Our routine is to leave all ideas out for discussion until the students are sure that a particular idea doesn't make sense. Thus, the following equations remained on the board even though I could not accept their logic.

Sarita

Equation	Justification
$8 \div \frac{1}{4} = 6$	8 people were served, they had 6 pints, and the picture shows fourths.
$6 \div \frac{1}{4} = 8$	[This was proposed in response to students who insisted that they couldn't accept the previous equation.]
$24 \div \frac{3}{4} = 8$ or 6	There are 24 pieces altogether, and each serving is $\frac{3}{4}$ of a pint, so there are 6 pints or 8 servings (depending on what you are looking for).
$\frac{3}{4} \div 8 = 6$	$\frac{3}{4}$ pint is the serving, there are 6 pints of ice cream, so 8 servings.

These last few equations do not make sense mathematically, nor do the justifications help them make sense. In some ways these were the easy equations to dismiss. For the last one, I might be persuaded to help this student reexamine whole-number division, because the justification seems clear—it just doesn't go with the equation.

My dilemma is that the first set of equations do not feel "right" to me even though they make mathematical sense. The $24 \div 3 = 8$ is disturbing. I see what the students mean, and I understand what they are doing; but these are whole numbers, and I think this is a fraction problem. Can it be both?

Where do I go from here? What do I do with my own thinking? What do I do to get the students to see this as a fraction division problem? Or do I? Who is confused, the students or me?

Stretching elastic

Selena

GRADE 6, NOVEMBER

For a recent homework assignment, students were asked to solve a
problem by drawing a diagram and writing an equation. When they
arrived in mathematics class the next day, I placed them randomly in
groups of two or three for a discussion of how everyone in their group
solved the problem. Part of the homework asked for alternative solutions
to the problem, so students knew that listening to other people's ideas
would help them finish the worksheet. They also knew that I would then
select a group of students to come to the board to explain how they
solved the problem. This was the problem we were working on:

? A piece of elastic can be stretched to $5\frac{1}{2}$ times its original
length. When fully stretched, it is 33 meters long. What was
the elastic's original length?

The first group to come to the board solved the problem this way.
They drew a diagram showing the length of the stretched elastic.

MARCUS: This is the 33 meters. We want to put them in $5\frac{1}{2}$ groups.

The group proceeded to separate the 33 meters of elastic into sections
$5\frac{1}{2}$ meters long.

45

50

55

60

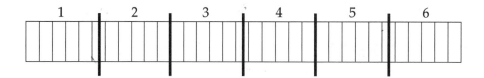

Before they could continue, hands all around the room flew into the air. Marcus called on Deena.

DEENA: I agree with the 6, but I disagree with what Marcus said.

TEACHER: What do you mean?

DEENA: I know what Marcus is doing, but I think he is all mixed up.

TEACHER: Can you say more about that?

I was not sure what Deena was thinking or what she was trying to articulate. It was difficult for her to express what she meant, but I wanted to give her the opportunity to explain her ideas.

DEENA: OK. The 6 is the answer. I know that because there are 6 groups. Marcus said that they put the 33 meters into $5\frac{1}{2}$ groups, but they didn't do that.

TEACHER: Can someone tell us in other words what Deena is saying?

AMIR: I think Deena is saying that Marcus's group said one thing but did another. It doesn't really matter.

PATRICE: But if it doesn't matter, where did the 6 come from anyway? You don't know about the 6 until you solve the problem.

FRANCINE: [*She is Marcus's partner*] We didn't know about the 6 until we finished with the groups. I think Marcus meant to say that we kept counting $5\frac{1}{2}$ pieces, or meters, until we ran out of meters. When we finished, we had 6 as the answer.

TEACHER: Six what?

MARCUS: Six meters. I see what they mean though. I didn't make $5\frac{1}{2}$ groups; I made 6 groups of $5\frac{1}{2}$.

TEACHER: Can the problem be solved if we made $5\frac{1}{2}$ groups?

The students quickly discussed this question and began drawing new diagrams on their papers. Many were excited to think that I may have provided them with the alternative solution they were required to include on their homework papers.

I wondered if the students would be able to think about the commutative property of $5\frac{1}{2}$ groups of 6 compared with 6 groups of $5\frac{1}{2}$. I also wondered what would happen with the half when students tried to create $5\frac{1}{2}$ groups. How would they think about the half, and how would they express the half in their diagram?

When the noise settled to a calm hum, I called on another group.

SONIA: The answer will be the same no matter which way you do the problem. It doesn't matter because $6 \times 5\frac{1}{2}$ is the same as $5\frac{1}{2} \times 6$. Both of those are 33. I suppose you want a picture?

Sonia is one of my more proficient mathematics students. She tends to be quick to understand, quick to formulate an answer, and usually not interested in drawing a diagram. However, I generally pretend I can accept nothing unless it can be proven with a diagram. So Sonia's group drew this on the board:

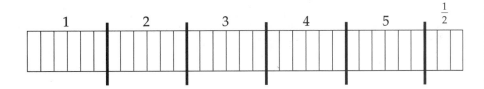

VICTOR: This picture shows $5\frac{1}{2}$ groups. There are 6 meters in each group except the last group. The last group only has 3 meters in it, because it is a half a group.

TEACHER: What about an equation? [*Sonia wrote two equations on the board.*]

$$33 \div 5\frac{1}{2} = 6 \qquad 33 \div 6 = 5\frac{1}{2}$$

DAPHNE: We didn't do it that way, but I think it is the same thing. We kept adding.

$$5\frac{1}{2} + 5\frac{1}{2} + 5\frac{1}{2} + 5\frac{1}{2} + 5\frac{1}{2} + 5\frac{1}{2} = 33$$

TEACHER: Is that the same, or is that different?

DAPHNE: It's a different way of doing the same thing. 115

ISAIAH: You could subtract also. Just keep doing subtraction until you have zero. Oh! You would have to subtract six times!

$$33 - 5\frac{1}{2} - 5\frac{1}{2} - 5\frac{1}{2} - 5\frac{1}{2} - 5\frac{1}{2} - 5\frac{1}{2}$$

The mathematics class was minutes from being over. Many of the students seemed to be thinking about the meaning of the operations division and multiplication. I knew that there were many things I would like to have them discuss. Having a fraction in the problem did not seem to pose much of an obstacle; I wondered if that was because the fraction was a half, and many students had a special way of thinking about halves that did not always carry over to other fractions. In the days to come, I hope to test this theory.

120

125

But of course, the students could not let me rest on my laurels too long. In the last two minutes of class Philip confronted me with a new wrinkle.

PHILIP: When I do this the *real* way, I get a different answer: 6 r 3. [*He came to the board to show us.*] The 3 is half of 6. So the remainder is the half.

130

$$5\frac{1}{2} \overline{)\begin{array}{r} 6\ r\ 3 \\ 33 \\ \underline{30} \\ 3 \end{array}}$$

As everyone left, I thought to myself, "Half of what?" Now what do I do? Is this my lesson for tomorrow?

135

C H A P T E R

8

Highlights of related research

by Lisa Yaffee

The cases in *Making Meaning for Operations* provide a glimpse of how children build an understanding of the four operations in classrooms where student thinking forms the basis of instruction. Although the story told by the cases is different in focus and in purpose from that conveyed by much of the formal educational research, the two accounts are complementary. Both teachers and researchers are trying to define the issues children confront as they struggle to make sense of mathematics. Teachers write specifically about intriguing aspects of their students' thinking or learning, whereas researchers often present ideas to support a theory or argument. Taken together, the cases and the research illuminate much of the rough conceptual terrain children must travel as they navigate among the features of the mathematical landscape. Our goal here is to weave these two genres together, so that each of many viewpoints contributes to the others. Having worked with a set of classroom narratives, we now turn to what various researchers say about how students come to understand addition, subtraction, multiplication, and division.

Modeling addition and subtraction

Children arrive at school with an intuitive understanding of mathematics. They are able to model and solve word problems without ever being taught how, using a variety of strategies.

Children derive informal mathematical knowledge from all aspects of their world. Setting the table, counting objects to compare quantities with someone else, pooling collections of items, creating and distributing equal shares of a coveted snack—these and other everyday experiences form the basis of the mathematical understandings children bring with them from home as they enter school. As Piaget (1965) and Dewey (1938) show, a young child's understanding of her environment is action-based, and doing provides the substance for learning. The same is true when children encounter word problems for the first time. Without being shown anything formal about adding, subtracting, multiplying, or dividing, children act out the events described in the problems they see (Carpenter & Moser, 1982; Carpenter, Moser, & Bebout, 1988; Hiebert & Behr, 1988; Baroody & Standifer, 1993; Resnick & Singer, 1993; Mack, 1993; Carpenter, Fennema & Franke, 1996).

5

10

Many of the actions children perform while solving addition and subtraction problems are derived from an understanding of counting and seem to develop along similar paths for most children. At first, students usually model all the quantities in a given problem by counting out objects to represent each distinct amount. Then they enact the problem situation by uniting or separating sets, finally counting the result. For example, when asked to solve the problem, "I have 6 rocks, and my friend gave me 8. How many do I have now?" children begin by directly modeling the action of the problem—putting out 6 objects to represent the first amount, 8 to represent the second, pushing the two sets together to form a single collection—then counting all the objects to get the total (Gelman & Gallistel, 1978; Steffe, von Glasersfeld, Richards, & Cobb, 1983; Fuson, 1992; Baroody & Standifer, 1993).

What children do with the objects they use for modeling mathematics situations reflects their understanding of the structure of the situation. In the word problem described above, for example, the structure of addition is understood from physically joining quantities. Contexts that adults would recognize as simple subtraction might be interpreted in several ways by children—as separating amounts, as building on, as a comparison of parts to wholes, or as a comparison of unrelated quantities, depending on the context (Carpenter et al., 1996; Fuson, 1992; Baroody & Standifer, 1993; Mack, 1993).

In a problem such as, "Electra has 14 rocks and loses 6 of them. How many does she have left?" many children assemble 14 items, remove 6, and count the remaining ones. Carpenter and colleagues (1996) call this action *separating,* a procedure traditionally used to teach subtraction. In a problem such as, "My friend has 6 rocks. After she picked up others, she had 14. How many more did she collect?" students often put out 6 objects, add some more until the grand total of 14 is reached, then go back and count the number of things added. In this case the action performed is *building on.* With a problem in which one person has 14 rocks, another has 6, and the question is how many more the first person has, many students place 14 uniform objects in one row and 6 in a row underneath so everything is aligned, then count the number of items in the row of 14 that stick out beyond the objects in the row of 6. The action performed here is *comparing,* in which children use a matching strategy in order to identify the "extra."

Although most conventionally schooled adults would probably call all the preceding situations "subtraction problems" and would represent each of them with the same equation, $14 - 6 = 8$, children often see these scenarios as qualitatively different from one another and solve each problem using a different action, as noted. The different actions performed by children highlight the distinct structures of various subtraction situations. Some researchers classify these structures as separate *problem types* (Carpenter et al., 1996; Baroody & Standifer, 1993).

After children have modeled many situations in which they represent with objects all of the amounts in an addition or subtraction problem, they eventually need to show only one of the quantities concretely. Initially students will represent the first quantity mentioned in a problem, counting up or back from that amount and keeping track of the number of counts made. Later they come to realize that it is easier to begin from the larger number and count on by the amount of the smaller one. In the case of the rock problems, while finding out how many rocks my friend and I have together if she has 6 and I have 8, someone might just count on from 8, putting up one finger to represent each of the rocks in the other person's portion, until six fingers are extended and six more numbers named. In the related subtraction scenario—my friend and I have 14 rocks together; if I have 6, how many does my friend have?—a student might start with 14 and count back 6, since this requires fewer steps than starting with 6 and counting up 8 (Gelman & Gallistel, 1978; Fuson, 1992; Carpenter et al., 1996).

These counting up and counting back strategies mark a turning away from direct modeling in that they require a more abstract concept of number than the earlier "show all quantities" methods do. Children must understand the idea of *cardinality*—in other words, that a number name or symbol stands for a constant amount, as well as a position in the counting sequence. For instance, when counting rocks, 6 not only names the sixth number counted and stands for the sixth stone reckoned, but it also represents the 5 additional stones previously included in the count (Fuson, 1992).

As well as knowing that a number always contains the same quantity, children must also understand that an addend is embedded in the sum at the same time that the two amounts exist separately. In other words, when considering $6 + 8 = 14$, children need to realize that 6 and 8 are parts of a larger whole as well as amounts in their own right. Finally, children must be able to count from anywhere in a sequence and hold a double count, keeping track of both the number of items they start with

Making Meaning for Operations

and the number that gets added or separated (Fuson, 1992). In Wendy's case 3 (chapter 1), Denisha knows that in order to determine how many girls are in school when two out of ten are absent, "You go down from 10 by 1, that's 9, and down 1 more, that's 8, so that's 2" (p. 11). This kindergartner is able to count backward correctly and monitor the number of counts made.

SECTION 2

Numerical reasoning begins

As students grow beyond the need to represent all of the amounts and actions in problems, they no longer rely entirely upon counting to determine the results of joining or separating sets, beginning instead to reason numerically about the quantities involved.

When children are able to pay attention to how all the amounts in a problem are related to one another, they can combine and separate them more flexibly. Students often use strategies based on facts they already know when they get to this stage. They take apart numbers and recombine them to form new quantities that they find easy to work with (Fuson, 1992). In Jody's case 10 (chapter 2), for example, Joachim changed 6 + 8 into (6 + 6) + 2, because he knows that 6 + 6 is 12 and that 6 + 8 must be 2 more than 12, since 8 is 2 more than 6. Joachim no longer relies upon counting when he needs to add. Another example is found in Melinda's case 9 (chapter 2). When asked to determine if a bag containing 16 pink cubes and 17 blue cubes has enough cubes for everyone in the class of 26 students, Nick figured like this: "Take 10 from the 16 and 10 from the 17. That's 20. Take the 6 from the 16, and now you have 26, enough for the class. The 7 from the 17 is left" (p. 38). Nick, like Joachim, solves the problem by breaking the involved quantities into amounts that are easier to think about and then reasons from there.

It is interesting that the growth from modeling all quantities and actions in a combining or separating problem to abstract reasoning with numbers is not a smooth or consistent transition for children. Some students appear to be at several levels simultaneously. Bella's kinder-gartners, for instance (case 6, chapter 1), are mostly still modeling every quantity in a problem and counting to get the total. At the same time, some are also shown grouping amounts in an array format, constructing 3 rows of 4 cubes each to represent the number of legs on three bunnies, which is a conventional representation for multiplication. They haven't begun to actually multiply and are still counting by ones to find their answers, but they are starting to expand their concept of addition to include the idea of combining equal groups.

Modeling multiplication and division

Although children come to an understanding of multiplication and division by modeling actions in a way similar to what they do for addition and subtraction, there are important and subtle differences.

One line of research suggests that children first encounter multiplication in the form of repeated addition, where several groups of the same size are combined (Fischbein, Deri, Nello, & Marino, 1985; Greer, 1992). Students again begin by modeling directly all the quantities and actions in a given problem. When trying to find out how many cans are in 3 six-packs of soda, for example, a child may first count out 6 objects, next count out 6 more, and then create a third group of 6, finally counting all to get a result. As children move beyond the need to show every item in a group of objects, they use a more abstract counting strategy, just as they do for addition and subtraction. However, instead of representing one amount and counting up or back from there, keeping track of the number of counts made, students might skip count to or back from a given number while tallying the number of counts (Carpenter et al., 1996).

In the addition or subtraction situation, students are counting individual objects, whereas in the multiplication or division scenario, they are counting both distinct objects and groups of objects. Thus, when adding the number of soda cans in 3 six-packs, a student may start at 6, count up 6 more to get 12 sodas with the second six-pack, and then count up 6 more to get a total of 18. In this case, the student is counting every soda can in each six-pack, 6, 7, 8, 9, 10, 11, 12, 13, 14, 15, 16, 17, 18. When multiplying, the child might put up one finger and count, "6," another and say "12," and a third finger, saying "18." In this latter case of skip counting, each of the three fingers raised represents a group of 6.

Later, according to this line of research, children are able to keep in mind all of the amounts in a multiplication or division problem and can break numbers up to use them flexibly (Carpenter et al., 1996). Examples of students making sense of division at this level of abstraction, as well as a glimpse of how difficult it is to keep track of whether one is counting single objects or groups of objects when multiplying, are found in Janine's case 15 (chapter 3). In this episode, three girls are trying to figure out how many packages holding 6 candy canes they would need so that each of 609 students could have one candy cane. Janine writes:

> Almost immediately the three decided that the problem had something to do with the 6 times tables—and that they had to go pretty far up the table to get to where they wanted to be. They started 6, 12, 18, 24, 30, and soon realized that there had to be a faster way. (p. 67)

One student knew that 6×9 was 54, so 6×90 would be 540.

> From 540 they decided that they had to add up by 6s to get to 609. . . . Letitia, after some thought, said that $540 + 10$ more would equal 600. One of the others said that $540 + 10$ is equal to 550 and not 600. Letitia struggled to explain. . . . She knew that 10 was important, but couldn't hold onto the idea that it wasn't 10 but *10 groups of 6* she was thinking about. (p. 67)

Letitia works this through, and her group decides that 90 packages and 10 more packages would provide 600 candy canes. Another package would bring them to 606, but they recognize that they would need still another package to supply 609 students with candy. Here, as in addition and subtraction, the children used relationships they already knew in making sense of multiplication and division situations.

Just as students come to understand multiplication as a form of repeated addition, they may understand division as a form of repeated subtraction. In case 13, for instance, Georgia's student Vanessa divides 8 into 24 by writing $24 - 8 = 16$, $16 - 8 = 8$, $8 - 8 = 0$, and then writes 3 for the answer. We can see, then, that some of these processes are similar to the modeling and counting strategies children use to figure out what addition and subtraction are.

However, multiplication and division are different from addition and subtraction in ways that aren't instantly apparent. Addition and subtraction situations involve numbers that count or measure amounts directly. Each number represents a set of something, a simple quantity. Problems are solved by joining, separating, or comparing sets, and the result is a third amount of the same kind as the other two: 3 donuts plus 4 donuts gives you 7 donuts (Schwartz, 1988; Hiebert & Behr, 1988; Dienes and Golding [1966] as cited by Harel & Confrey, 1994).

Multiplication, though, frequently involves two factors that represent different kinds of things. Three bags each contain 4 donuts; how many donuts do I have? One factor is the number of sets, whereas the other is the number of items per set; both of these amounts must be tracked. The result is the quantity of donuts in all three bags, or in other words, the items contained in a set of sets (Harel & Confrey, 1994).

To understand the idea of a set of sets, the child must be able to conceive of a collection as a *unit* (Harel & Confrey, 1994). In Bella's case 6 (chapter 1), we see at least two children working with this idea as they represent the number of eggs there would be in three baskets, each containing 3 eggs.

> Jenna used the Unifix cubes. First she made a unit of 3 cubes and brought them over to show me. I asked her what she had, and she said that she had one basket.
>
> "Where are the other baskets?" I asked.
>
> "I haven't made them yet," she said, heading back to the table. Soon she was back again, this time with two units of 3.
>
> "How many baskets do you have now?" (p. 24)

Jenna knows she has made two baskets and needs to make one more, which she goes off to do. Although she won't know how many eggs are in her three baskets until she counts them, she does realize that each group of 3 comprises a unit, namely one basket, and that each basket contains 3 items. Junior, on the other hand, is still building this idea. His

Making Meaning for Operations

model of the same problem consists of 3 orange cubes, 3 white cubes, and 3 yellow cubes. He knows he has three baskets, each containing 3 individual eggs, but when his teacher asks how many eggs he has in all, he says, "Three." Bella writes:

> Junior showed me how he counted: Each unit of 3 was "one" to him. I took one unit and broke it apart. He counted them, "1, 2, 3," and agreed that they represented 3 eggs. I put them back together with the other two units of 3 and asked him how many eggs were there. Again, he said "Three." I tried several ways to help him see that I wanted him to count the individual cubes, but it didn't help. He was unable to see the difference or sameness between cubes once they became a single unit of 3. (pp. 24–25)

Whereas Jenna seems to understand the idea of a set of sets, Junior is still trying to figure out how one unit can be comprised of multiple items and yet maintain its identity as both a single entity and as a collection of entities.

To summarize, then, one line of the research literature suggests that children first come to understand multiplication as a form of repeated addition, derived from experience with counting as just described, and then go on to construct other meanings for it later, as we shall see. Much of this research tries to define types of multiplication and division problems and examines student problem solving as it relates to those types. We will look at these ideas more closely in the next section of this essay. However, there is another group of researchers who find that students' ideas about multiplication and division develop not out of counting, but rather from experiences with *sharing*, in which equal portions must be created. It is in dealing out these "fair shares" that children come to understand ratio, multiplication, and division as inextricably related concepts, inherent in the same situations. They are doing this, in many cases, while still working on higher number counts and while sorting out addition and subtraction concepts (Confrey & Harel, 1994; Confrey, 1995).

Consider, for example, the problem MaryAnn's fourth-grade students were working on in February (case 20, chapter 5): "I invited 8 people to my party (including me), and I only had 3 brownies. How much did each

person get if they had fair shares?" Maribel still models directly the
actions of the problem, using pictures to create and allocate her portions:

> For example . . . she drew 8 faces for the 8 people at the party
> and drew 3 brownies which she cut into eighths. She then
> began distributing the pieces to the people. Each time she
> distributed 8 pieces, she crossed out the brownie they came
> from. After she finished distributing the pieces, she counted
> them up. "They each get $\frac{3}{8}$," she wrote. (p. 89)

Maribel understands that this method results in equal groups, and she
knows that the people in the problem have fair shares without having to
count the portions. Although she uses counting to verify her solution, the
actions she uses to solve the problem seem not to be rooted in counting
nor, by extension, in repeated subtraction. Instead, they could derive from
an independent action which Confrey and her colleagues call "splitting,"
the basic structures of which are halving and doubling (Confrey & Harel,
1994; Confrey, 1988, 1995).

Although we don't see Maribel halving and doubling quantities in
order to solve multiplication and division problems, thereby working out
an understanding of what those operations mean, the DMI cases provide
many examples of students doing just that. In *Building a System of Tens*,
we see a majority of Eleanor's students halving and doubling to solve the
equation 27×4 (case 18, chapter 5). Stephan explains his process clearly:

> First way: I used my head only. I added 27 and 27 and I got 54,
> then I added 54 and 54 and I got the answer 108. I added 27
> and 27 because I knew it was half of 4×27, so I put the two
> halves together and I got 108. (*Building a System of Tens*, p. 73)

In Georgia's case 13 (*Making Meaning for Operations*, chapter 3), Cory
is trying to figure out how many bookshelves Joni can make if she uses
4 boards for each and starts with 36 boards. His teacher writes:

> Cory knew that 36 is made up of 30 and 6, and half of 30 is
> 15, and half of 6 is 3. Then he knew that 15 plus 3 is 18. He
> understands division in terms of halving, as he clearly states:
> "Divided by is half of whatever the number is." . . . And he
> knows that dividing by 4 is like halving twice. (p. 61)

A couple of months later, Georgia's students are still halving and doubling while figuring out what half of a half is (case 23, chapter 6). Justine explains:

> "[The whole] would be split into 4 pieces. It's already into 2 pieces, and then if you split it into 4 pieces, then you make each half in half. . . . I think I've done fractions before because I know when you split something in half it's twice as much. . . . And if you did eighths in half, it would be sixteenths, and so on. . . . Then thirty-twoths, and sixty-fourths." (pp. 110–111)

Justine and her classmates see halving and doubling as the same process, which supports Confrey's contention that multiplication, division, and ratio coevolve (Confrey, personal communication, February 3, 1997).

Making meaning for multiplication and division

As children sort out the various contexts that can be modeled by multiplication and division, they continue to work on understanding the different types of units in these problems, deepening their knowledge of how the operations work and what they mean.

As mentioned earlier, one branch of the research literature (the one which suggests that children first come to understand multiplication as a form of repeated addition and division as repeated subtraction) examines student problem solving as it relates to the type of problems being explored. Two distinct types of multiplication situations have been categorized, each of which is related to a division situation as well. We discuss the two types of multiplication and their related division separately, the same way this research typically examines them.

We have already described one type of multiplication, in which the two factors represent different kinds of things—one, the number of sets, and the other, the number of items per set. Kouba and Franklin (1993) call this type of multiplication *asymmetrical,* because the multiplier and multiplicand play different roles and cannot be interchanged. As mentioned earlier, with the multiplication problem "3 bags, each containing 4 donuts; how many donuts do I have?" the two factors can't be used in place of one another. Three bags containing 4 donuts each $(4 + 4 + 4)$ is a different situation from 4 bags of 3 donuts each $(3 + 3 + 3 + 3)$, even though both involve 12 donuts. If one person gets each bag, in the first case fewer people eat more donuts; in the second, more people eat fewer donuts. Because the two factors represent distinct types of units, the related division situation can be defined in two ways (Fischbein et al., 1985; Greer, 1992; Kouba & Franklin, 1993).

In one type of related division, known in the research literature as *partitive* and commonly called *dealing,* an amount is split evenly between a certain number of groups. An example of this sort of "equal sharing" problem (Greer's term, 1992) might be this: "You have 12 donuts to share equitably among 3 children. How many could each child have?" The result is the number of items in each group or portion. In the other kind of related division problem, known as *quotitive* or *measure* and commonly called *grouping,* a quantity is split into shares of a certain size and the result is the number of groups obtained: "You have 12 donuts. You want to make bags containing 3 donuts each. How many bags can you make?" Though both problems can be solved using the same division equation, $12 \div 3 = 4$, the solution to the first problem would be 4 donuts for each of 3 people, whereas the answer to the second would be 4 bags with 3 donuts in each.

Children usually represent and solve these two types of problems differently. For a quotitive situation like the one in which 12 donuts are packed in bags of 3, the number of donuts in each group is known and the number of groups is sought. To solve, students typically count out 12 objects and then put them in piles of 3 until they run out (Kouba & Franklin, 1993; Carpenter et al., 1996). Beyond the direct modeling stage, students might skip count (3, 6, 9, 12) to find out how many groups of 3 are in 12, or rely on their knowledge of multiplication facts (Carpenter et al., 1996). Here, our classroom narratives contribute even greater detail to the research picture, since Georgia's students, in case 13, come up with other methods: repeatedly subtracting 3 from 12 until there isn't anything left to subtract from; adding 3 to itself to get 6 and then adding 6 to itself to get 12; setting up a chart showing that 1 bag contains 3 donuts, 2 bags contain 6, 3 bags contain 9, and 4 bags would contain 12. Though the first method could be based on counting, the last two might be considered "splitting" strategies, among possible interpretations.

When working on the partitive version of that same situation, "If 3 people are sharing 12 donuts, how many donuts does each get?" children use several direct modeling methods. The most common is to select 12 items and then deal them one by one into 3 piles until they run out, counting the number in each group to get the answer. Another approach is to count out 12 objects to represent donuts, guess at a number that could go to each child, then deal out that many to see if any are left, and modify the initial guess if needed. A third method is not to count out the total to begin with, but simply to create 3 groups of an arbitrary size, keeping track of how many objects are used up, until the total of 12 is reached (Kouba & Franklin, 1993). There are, of course, more abstract strategies as well—guessing an amount to skip count by and seeing if it reaches 12, then adjusting the guess accordingly so that 3 counts are obtained; or using known multiplication facts (Carpenter et al., 1996).

The second type of multiplication described through this line of research is called *symmetrical* by Kouba and Franklin (1993), because both factors play the same role, represent the same type of unit, and can be interchanged. One of the most common instances of symmetrical multiplication is area; the length of a rectangle might be 4 feet and the width 3 feet until you rotate the figure 90 degrees, when the length then becomes 3 feet and the width 4 feet. The same symmetry is true of the array model. If you have a box of chocolates arranged in 3 rows and 4 columns, you can turn the box at a 90 degree angle and then have 4 rows and 3 columns. Another symmetrical form has been called *cross product* or *Cartesian product multiplication,* an example of which is this: "If you own 4 shirts and 3 pairs of pants, how many different outfits can you put together?" (Greer, 1992).

Because the factors are interchangeable in these scenarios, there is only one type of related division, in which a missing factor is determined. For example, if the area allotted for the rectangular third-grade garden is 12 square feet, and we've already put 3 feet of fence along one side, how much fence will we need for a side perpendicular to the first? Although the factors in a symmetrical multiplication problem are the same kind of unit (items of clothing, linear feet of fence), the result of such multiplication is a unit different from that of the factors. *Items of clothing* times *items of clothing* become *outfits,* and *linear feet* times *linear feet* become *square feet* (Kouba & Franklin, 1993; Greer, 1992).

S E C T I O N   5

Encountering fractions in sharing situations

As children model and solve problems that involve sharing quantities fairly, they encounter a new type of number: fractions.

There is much evidence to suggest that children explore sharing problems and begin to build fraction concepts before they reach school (Hunting & Davis, 1991; Hunting & Sharpley, 1988; Empson, 1995; Piaget, 1965). The line of research which holds that ideas about multiplication and division first emerge from counting structures, like repeated addition and subtraction, also observes that fractions come out of sharing situations where there is material remaining, as well as where the number of sharers is greater than the amount to be shared (Empson, 1995; Hunting & Davis, 1991).

An example of the first situation, in which children figure out what to do with the leftovers after dealing out items to share equally, is provided by Janie's case 24 in *Building a System of Tens*. There April divides 143 jelly beans among 8 students, finding that each person would get 17 candies with 7 left over. Janie writes:

> Then she came up with a way to divide up the 7 extra jelly beans. She took 4 of them and divided each in half, so each of the 8 kids got $\frac{1}{2}$. Then she had 3 left over, so she took 2 of those and divided them into fourths, so each kid got an additional $\frac{1}{4}$. Then she divided the last jelly bean into eighths, so each kid got another $\frac{1}{8}$. Now the question was, How much was $\frac{1}{2} + \frac{1}{4} + \frac{1}{8}$? (*Building a System of Tens*, p. 98)

April resolves this by drawing a circle showing $\frac{1}{2}$, $\frac{1}{4}$, and $\frac{1}{8}$ inside of it. From this she can tell there was $\frac{1}{8}$ of the circle unaccounted for, so each child would finally end up with $17\frac{7}{8}$ jelly beans. April, a fourth grader, obviously has much prior experience with dividing up quantities. She has already internalized the ideas that all the material needs to be used up and that everyone needs to have the same-sized share, two concepts that children don't automatically bring to partitioning tasks (Hunting & Davis, 1991; Hunting & Sharpley, 1988).

Children also encounter fractions in whole-number division contexts in which the number of people sharing exceeds the quantity of items to be shared. MaryAnn's students (cases 18 and 19) misread the problem $39 \div 5$ as "5 divided by 39" and then try to make sense of this latter statement. At first they see the two equations as synonymous, a phenomenon well represented in the research literature, and then go on to claim, "You can't divide a number that's lower by one that's higher" (p. 79), an idea forged by years of experience with whole-number operations, and one that has also received research attention (Graeber & Baker, 1992). Several months later when they revisit this problem at the next grade level, the children are able to visualize what 5 divided by 39 looks like by thinking about 5 candy bars shared among 39 people. Creating a context helps students see that "they would have to cut the 5 candy bars into little equal pieces" (p. 84); and "each person would only get a really small piece, not anywhere like a whole candy bar" (p. 85).

S E C T I O N 6

Understanding fractional amounts

When students begin to operate on fractions and other rational numbers, they need to perceive these new numbers as quantities in order to make sense of what fractions mean.

Although we see MaryAnn's students working to understand what fractions are and how they behave, much of the basic research about how children make sense of rational numbers has a different focus. This work was done mostly in the 1980s and dealt predominantly with middle-school and older children who spent many years in traditional classrooms, where memorizing the rules and procedures for solving computation problems formed the bulk of the mathematics program. The consequences of such instruction are visible in the research, which examines patterns of errors made by students, reflecting common "misconceptions." The overwhelming impression is of children who have lost the ability, even the desire, to make sense of the mathematics they are doing, a picture that stands in sharp contrast to some of the current research conducted in classrooms like MaryAnn's. So, with these cautionary words that much of the seminal work about children and fractions focuses on what students can't do and don't know, rather than on what ideas are in place and which ones are still under construction, we turn now, in the final two sections of this essay, to what the literature says is hard for children to understand about fractions.

Even though addition and subtraction of rational numbers still involve joining, separating, and comparing amounts, just as for whole numbers, Carpenter found in some of his earlier work that students don't see fractions as quantities, "but see them as four separate whole numbers to be combined in some fashion" (Carpenter [1976] as cited by Vinner, Hershkowitz, & Bruckheimer, 1981). This finding was confirmed by the second National Assessment of Educational Progress, in which students were asked to pick an estimate for $\frac{12}{13} + \frac{7}{8}$ from the choices 1, 2, 19, and 21. Most students chose the latter two, presumably combining either numerators or denominators together. Following whole-number addition procedures grown comfortable from years of rote usage, students lost the sense of $\frac{12}{13}$ and $\frac{7}{8}$ as quantities close to 1 (Behr, Wachsmuth, & Post, 1985).

This attempt to fit addition and subtraction of fractions into existing models for whole-number computation is a common occurrence among students. Behr's group (1985), Carpenter and colleagues (1976), and Howard (1991) all saw children join and separate numerators with numerators and denominators with denominators, as if the numerators and denominators in each fraction bore no relation to one another. In MaryAnn's case 20, we see Jackson begin to fall into the same trap but then extricate himself as his understanding of the meaning of fractions kicks in. While determining how much brownie a person gets if she receives $\frac{1}{4}$ of one, $\frac{1}{4}$ of another, and $\frac{1}{8}$ of a third, Jackson says:

> I was adding the 1 + 1 + 1 [from the numerators] and it came
> to 3, but then I went to add the bottoms [4 + 4 + 8] and it
> didn't make sense. There's nothing here [in the problem]
> that's 16, and the numbers I was getting wouldn't match the
> brownies. . . . I know the $\frac{1}{4}$ and $\frac{1}{4}$ make $\frac{1}{2}$, and then $\frac{1}{8}$. So . . .
> each person had a share of $\frac{1}{2}$ and $\frac{1}{8}$ (p. 93)

By focusing on the quantities the fractions signify, Jackson realizes that his original approach to solving the problem makes no sense.

Most of the time when we combine fractions, we add together numbers which are expressed as parts of the same-sized implied whole. In other words, when thinking about Jackson's $\frac{1}{2} + \frac{1}{8}$, we assume both portions to have come from brownies of equivalent size. Since the $\frac{1}{2}$ and the $\frac{1}{8}$ are defined relative to the same whole, they can therefore be understood as $\frac{4}{8} + \frac{1}{8}$. This idea of comprehending what the unit is—of knowing that when you add $\frac{1}{2}$ of something to $\frac{1}{8}$ of something, you are putting together quantities that are understood in relation to a third amount, the whole or unit—is difficult for children to grasp.

Addition and subtraction of fractions can be further complicated for children by the fact that familiar, real-life situations exist, when dealing with ratios, in which adding numerators or denominators together is appropriate. For example, batting averages are computed by adding all the season's hits and dividing them by all the times at bat. If you get 5 hits in 8 times at bat during your first game, and 1 hit in 6 times at bat during your second game, then you are batting 6 for 14, or about .429. Field goal percentages in hockey, soccer, and basketball are figured the same way—the total goals made per total attempted shots over the course of the season. In another scenario, if one pitcher of punch contains 2 cups of juice and 3 cups of ginger ale, and a second contains 4 cups of juice and 6 of cups ginger ale, when you combine them, the new punch will have 6 cups of juice and 9 cups of ginger ale (Howard, 1991).

Revising ideas for operations with fractions

As the domain of number expands beyond whole numbers and into the rationals, the ideas children have about operations, especially multiplication and division, frequently need revision.

When students move beyond addition and subtraction and into multiplication and division of rational numbers, their whole-number interpretations of those operations, especially if they are based on counting structures, need revision. Repeated addition, for example, which makes sense when modeling multiplication of whole numbers, doesn't seem to work as well for multiplying rationals. In whole-number repeated addition, children combine quantities more than one whole time, and the amounts they end up with are always larger than those they started with. Repeated addition of rationals, though, is hard to comprehend. When considering $\frac{2}{10} \times \frac{1}{2}$ as repeated addition, what does it mean to add $\frac{1}{2}$ to itself $\frac{2}{10}$ of a time? Students need problem contexts that are meaningful, as well as situations which help them see that multiplication no longer necessarily results in a number larger than either of the quantities operated upon (Hiebert & Behr, 1988).

Graeber and Campbell (1993) suggest that an area model works well for illustrating multiplication of rationals, but that students first need to understand this model in connection with whole-number multiplication. Even with lots of previous whole-number experience, children still have to work hard to make sense of how to compute the area of a rectangle with rational number sides. Sarita's students in case 25, for instance, have found the areas of countless rectangles with whole-number dimensions, but when determining the area of a rectangle that has a width of $2\frac{3}{4}$ and the length of $3\frac{2}{3}$, it takes a while for them to realize that they "could indeed find the area of the entire region by taking all the things that [they] had counted," namely $2\frac{3}{4}$ rows of $3\frac{2}{3}$ units each, "and adding them together" (p. 113).

When children encounter division of rationals, their whole-number notions of that operation are also challenged. Smaller numbers can now be divided by larger—contrary to what many students believe is possible, until they are shown contexts in which this would make sense, as, for example, when $\frac{1}{2}$ of a pizza is shared by 4 people (Graeber & Campbell, 1993; Graeber & Tanenhaus, 1993). Another conception about division that needs revising when dealing with rational numbers is the idea that division always "makes things smaller." In fact, the opposite is now true, as in the problem Sarita gave her students in case 27:

> You are giving a birthday party. From Ben and Jerry's ice cream factory, you order 6 pints of ice cream. If you serve $\frac{3}{4}$ of a pint of ice cream to each guest, how many guests can be served?

In this case the answer is actually larger than either of the numbers operated upon.

None of Sarita's students represent what's happening in the ice cream problem with a division with fractions equation—an outcome that puzzles their teacher. The children base their choice of operation on what they perceive the mathematical structure of the situation to be, rather than on the type or size of the numbers used, as the children in research studies often did. For example, one of Sarita's pupils took the 6 pints of ice cream and split them into $\frac{4}{4}$ each. That created "24 pieces, 3 pieces to a serving, 8 people can be served" (p. 127). The action performed by this student was grouping the 24 pieces by 3s, a division procedure, described by the equation $24 \div 3 = 8$.

By contrast, children in numerous studies of classrooms in which computation procedures were the focus of instruction chose operations for problem solving based on the size or type of the numbers involved, instead of on the situation being modeled by the problem (Greer, 1987, 1992; Bell, Fischbein, & Greer, 1984; Bell, Swan, & Taylor, 1981; Fischbein et al., 1985). For instance, when given two problems with exactly the same mathematical structure but with different types of numbers, Ekenstam and Greger found that 12- and 13-year-olds picked multiplication to solve one and division to solve the other (Ekenstam and Greger [1983] as cited by Greer, 1992). The first problem, which they solved by multiplication, asked how much 5 kg of cheese cost if 1 kg costs 28 kroner. The second problem, which they solved by division, was essentially the same: How much would 0.923 kg of cheese cost if 1 kg costs 27.5 kroner? "It seems clear that the choice of division for the second problem is based on the realization that the answer will be less than 27.50, combined with the belief that multiplication always makes bigger, and division smaller" (Greer, 1992, p. 288).

Conclusion

Although much of the research described in this essay, as noted previously, was conducted with children whose school mathematics experiences emphasized mastery of computation rather than making sense of number and operations, this work is what informs our current understanding of how mathematics concepts are built. There is still much to learn. Increasingly, the studies being done now focus on classrooms like those described in the cases, where students are presented with problems to interpret and model in ways that make sense to them. As contexts are created to help children understand how different types of numbers and operations represent real-life situations, we are able to glimpse the complex process by which students internalize the mathematical structures of the problems they encounter. Though we may not fully understand this process, we can still recognize and support children as they move toward making meaning for the operations.

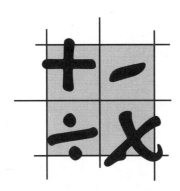

References

Baroody, A. J., & Standifer, D. J. (1993). Addition and subtraction in the primary grades. In R. J. Jensen (Ed.), *Research ideas for the classroom, early childhood* (pp. 72–102). New York: Macmillan.

Behr, M., Wachsmuth, I., & Post, T. R. (1985). Construct a sum: A measure of children's understanding of fraction size. *Journal for Research in Mathematics Education, 16,* 120–131.

Bell, A., Fischbein, E., & Greer, B. (1984). Choice of operation in verbal arithmetic problems: The effects of number size, problem structure, and context. *Educational Studies in Mathematics, 15,* 129–147.

Bell, A., Swan, M., & Taylor, G. (1981). Choice of operations in verbal problems with decimal numbers. *Educational Studies in Mathematics, 12,* 399–420.

Carpenter, T. P., & Moser, J. M. (1982). The development of addition and subtraction problem-solving skills. In T. P. Carpenter, J. M. Moser, & T. A. Romberg (Eds.), *Addition and subtraction: A cognitive perspective* (pp. 9–24). Hillsdale, NJ: Erlbaum.

Carpenter, T. P., Fennema, E., & Franke, M. (1996). Cognitively guided instruction: A knowledge base for reform in primary mathematics instruction. *Elementary School Journal, 1,* 3–20.

Carpenter, T. P., Moser, J. M., & Bebout, H. C. (1988). Representation of addition and subtraction word problems. *Journal for Research in Mathematics Education, 19,* 345–357.

Confrey, J., & Harel, G. (1994). Introduction. In G. Harel & J. Confrey (Eds.), *The development of multiplicative reasoning in the learning of mathematics* (pp. vii–xxviii). Albany, NY: State University of New York Press.

Confrey, J. (1988). Multiplication and splitting: Their role in under-standing exponential functions. *Proceedings of the 10th Annual Meeting of the North American Chapter of the International Group for the Psychology of Mathematics Education,* 250–259.

Confrey, J. (1995). Student voice in examining "splitting" as an approach to ratio, proportions, and fractions. In L. Meira & W. Carrher (Eds.), *Proceedings of the 19th International Conference for the Psychology of Mathematics Education, 1,* 3–29. Recife, Brazil: Universidade Federal do Pernambuco.

Dewey, J. (1938). *Education and experience.* New York: Macmillan.

Empson, S. B. (1995). *Equal sharing and shared meaning: The development of fraction concepts in a first-grade classroom.* Paper presented at the annual meeting of the American Educational Research Association, San Francisco, CA.

Fischbein, E., Deri, M., Nello, M. S., & Marino, M. S. (1985). The role of implicit models in solving verbal problems in multiplication and division. *Journal for Research in Mathematics Education, 16,* 3–17.

Fuson, K. C. (1992). Research on whole number addition and subtraction. In D. A. Grouws (Ed.), *Handbook of research on mathematics teaching and learning* (pp. 243–275). New York: Macmillan.

Gelman, R., & Gallistel, C. R. (1978). *The child's understanding of number.* Cambridge, MA: Harvard University Press.

Graeber, A. O., & Baker, K. M. (1992). Little into big is the way it always is. *Arithmetic Teacher, 37,* 18–21.

Graeber, A. O., & Campbell, P. F. (1993). Misconceptions about multipli-cation and division. *Arithmetic Teacher, 40,* 408–411.

Graeber, A. O. & Tanenhaus, E. (1993). Multiplication and division: From whole numbers to rational numbers. In D. T. Owens (Ed.), *Research ideas for the classroom, middle grades mathematics* (pp. 99–136). New York: Macmillan.

Greer, B. (1987). Nonconservation of multiplication and division involving decimals. *Journal for Research in Mathematics Education, 18,* 37–45.

Greer, B. (1992). Multiplication and division as models of situations. In D. A. Grouws (Ed.), *Handbook of research on mathematics teaching and learning* (pp. 276–295). New York: Macmillan.

Harel, G., & Confrey, J. (1994). *The development of multiplicative reasoning in the learning of mathematics.* Albany, NY: State University of New York Press.

Hiebert, J. & Behr, M. (1988). Introduction. In J. Hiebert & M. Behr (Eds.), *Number concepts and operations in the middle grades* (pp. 1–18). Hillsdale, NJ and Reston, VA: Erlbaum & National Council of Teachers of Mathematics.

Howard, A. (1991). Addition of fractions—The unrecognized problem. *Mathematics Teacher, 84,* 710–713.

Hunting, R. P., & Davis, G. E. (1991). Dimensions of young children's conceptions of the fraction ½. In R. P. Hunting & G. E Davis (Eds.), *Early fraction learning* (pp. 27–53). New York: Springer-Verlag.

Hunting, R. P., & Sharpley, C. F. (1988). Preschoolers' cognitions of fractional units. *British Journal of Educational Psychology, 58,* 172–183.

Kouba, V. L., & Franklin, K. (1993). Multiplication and division: Sense making and meaning. In R. J. Jensen (Ed.), *Research ideas for the classroom, early childhood* (pp. 103–126). New York: Macmillan.

Mack, N. (1993). Learning rational numbers with understanding: The case of informal knowledge. In T. P. Carpenter, E. Fennema, & T. Romberg (Eds.), *Rational numbers: An integration of research* (pp. 85–105). Hillsdale, NJ: Erlbaum.

Piaget, J. (1965). *The child's conception of the world.* Totowa, NJ: Littlefield, Adams.

Resnick, L. B., & Singer, J. A. (1993). Protoquantitative origins of ratio reasoning. In T. Carpenter, E. Fennema, & T. Romberg (Eds.), *Rational numbers: An integration of research* (pp. 107–130). Hillsdale, NJ: Erlbaum.

Schwartz, J. L. (1988). Intensive quantity and referent transforming arithmetic operations. In J. Hiebert & M. Behr. (Eds.), *Number concepts and operations in the middle grades* (pp. 41–52). Hillsdale, NJ: Erlbaum.

Steffe, L. P., von Glasersfeld, E., Richards, J., & Cobb, P. (1983). *Children's counting types: Philosophy, theory, and application.* New York: Praeger.

Vinner, S., Hershkowitz, R., & Bruckheimer, M. (1981). Some cognitive factors as causes of mistakes in the addition of fractions. *Journal for Research in Mathematics Education,* 70–76.